THE COMPLETE WRITER

Level One
Workbook for Writing with Ease

TEACHER EDITION

By

Susan Wise Bauer

and

Peter Buffington

Peace Hill Press
18021 The Glebe Lane
Charles City, VA 23030
www.peacehillpress.com

This workbook is to be used in conjunction with
THE COMPLETE WRITER: WRITING WITH EASE
Strong Fundamentals

ISBN   978-1-933339-25-2

Available at www.peacehillpress.com or
wherever books are sold

Artwork by *Jeff West*
Cover design by *Mike Fretto*
Interior design and page layout by
Electronic Publishing Services, Inc., Tennessee

Publisher's Cataloging-In-Publication Data
(Prepared by The Donohue Group, Inc.)

Bauer, Susan Wise.
    Level 1 workbook for Writing with ease / by Susan Wise Bauer and Peter Buffington.

    p. : ill. ; cm.—(Complete writer)

    "This book is to be used in conjunction with The Complete writer: writing with ease:
strong fundamentals."— t.p. verso.
    Includes bibliographical references
    ISBN: 978-1-933339-26-9

    1. English language—Rhetoric—Problems, exercises, etc. 2. English
language—Composition and exercises. I. Buffington, Peter. II. Bauer, Susan
Wise. Writing with ease. III. Title. IV. Title: Workbook for Writing with ease. Level 1

    LB1576 .B381 2008   *Level 1*
    372.62/3   2007940223

CONTENTS

READING SELECTIONS

Week 1: *Little House in the Big Woods*, by Laura Ingalls Wilder

Week 2: *The Adventures of Pinocchio*, by Carlo Collodi

Week 3: "Rumpelstiltzkin," from *The Blue Fairy Book*, by Andrew Lang

Week 4: *Alice's Adventures in Wonderland*, by Lewis Carroll

Week 5: "The Frog Prince," by Jacob and Wilhelm Grimm, translated by Edgar Taylor and Marian Edwardes

Week 6: *Mary Poppins*, by P.L. Travers

Week 7: *Peter Rabbit*, by Beatrix Potter

Week 8: *Caddie Woodlawn*, by Carol Ryrie Brink

Week 9: *Charlotte's Web*, by E.B. White

Week 10: *Davy Crockett, Young Rifleman*, by Aileen Wells Parks, and *Sacagawea: American Pathfinder*, by Flora Warren Seymour

Week 11: *The Trumpet of the Swan*, by E.B. White

Week 12: "Today is Monday" (poem) and "Old Mother Hubbard" (poem)

Week 13: *The Saturdays*, by Elizabeth Enright

Week 14: "Bed in Summer" (poem), by Robert Louis Stevenson, and a traditional folk tale, adapted for this book by Susan Wise Bauer

Week 15: *The Railway Children*, by Edith Nesbit

Week 16: "Master of All Masters," by Joseph Jacobs, and "The Dog and His Reflection," by Aesop

Week 17: *The Reluctant Dragon*, by Kenneth Grahame

Week 18: *Winnie-the-Pooh*, by A.A. Milne, and *The House at Pooh Corner*, by A.A. Milne

Week 19: *The Light Princess*, by George MacDonald

Week 20: *A Child's Geography of the World*, by V.M. Hillyer

Week 21: *Tom Sawyer*, by Mark Twain

Week 22: *The Velveteen Rabbit*, Margery Williams Bianco (sometimes listed as Margery Williams)

Week 23: *How to Eat Fried Worms*, by Thomas Rockwell

Week 24: *The Happy Hollisters* by Jerry West

Week 25: *Pollyanna*, by Eleanor Porter

Week 26: *The Tale of Benjamin Bunny*, by Beatrix Potter

Week 27: *A Christmas Carol*, by Charles Dickens

Week 28: *Little House on the Prairie*, by Laura Ingalls Wilder

Week 29: *All-of-a-Kind Family*, by Sydney Taylor

Week 30: "The Crocodile and the Monkey," from *The Giant Crab and Other Tales from Old India*, by W.H.D. Rouse.

Week 31: "The Sandpiper," by Celia Thaxter, and "The Nightingale and the Glow-worm," by William Cowper

Week 32: "Sir Gawain and the Green Knight," from *King Arthur and His Knights of the Round Table*, by Roger Lancelyn Green

Week 33: *Charlie and the Chocolate Factory*, by Roald Dahl

Week 34: *Socks*, by Beverly Cleary

Week 35: *The Wind in the Willows*, by Kenneth Grahame

Week 36: "Rain," from *A Child's Garden of Verses*, by Robert Louis Stevenson, and *The Wonderful Wizard of Oz*, by L. Frank Baum

WEEK 1

DAY ONE: The First Copywork Exercise   *Student Page 1*

Focus: *Beginning capitals and ending periods*

Pull out Student Page 1. Write the student's name and the date for him as he watches, or ask him to write the name and date independently. The following two model sentences are already printed on it:

> There were no roads.
> The deer and the rabbits would be shy and swift.

Ask the student to look carefully at the sentences. While he is examining the sentences, explain that these sentences are from the first chapter of *Little House in the Big Woods*, by Laura Ingalls Wilder. *Little House* is about a family that lives in Wisconsin in the 1860s, in a deep forest where few others live. Ask the student to point out the capital letters that begin the sentences, and the periods that end them. Tell him that both of these are **complete sentences**.

Choose whichever sentence is appropriate to the student's handwriting ability and ask the student to copy it on the lines provided. Watch the student; if he begins to make an error, gently stop him and ask him to look at the model again. Always allow him to erase errors in order to correct them.

Remember that it is not necessary to copy both sentences. A shorter and longer option are provided because the fine motor skills of very young writers span a wide range of development.

DAY TWO: The First Narration Exercise   *Student Page 2*

Pull out Student Page 2. Write the student's name and the date for him as he watches, or ask him to write the name and date independently.

Read the following passage out loud to the student:

> Once upon a time, sixty years ago, a little girl lived in the Big Woods of Wisconsin, in a little gray house made of logs.
>
> The great, dark trees of the Big Woods stood all around the house, and beyond them were other trees and beyond them were more trees. As far as a man could go to the north in a day, or a week, or a whole month, there was nothing but woods. There were no houses. There were no roads. There were no people. There were only trees and the wild animals who had their homes among them.
>
> —From *Little House in the Big Woods*
> by Laura Ingalls Wilder

Ask the following questions. Remind the student to answer you in complete sentences. If he answers in a fragment, turn the fragment into a complete sentence, say it to him, and then ask him to repeat this sentence back to you. If he cannot answer a question, read him the part of the passage that contains the answer, and then ask the question again.

Instructor: How many years ago does this story happen?
Student: *This story happens sixty years ago.* [If necessary, you can explain to the student that this book was written in the 1920s. When Laura Ingalls Wilder was writing this first chapter, her childhood in the 1860s was sixty years ago. Now, we would say that the story happened almost 150 years ago!]

Instructor: Where did the little girl live?
Student: *She lived in Wisconsin OR in the big woods of Wisconsin.*

Instructor: If a man went north for a whole month, what would he find?
Student: *He would find more woods.*

Instructor: There were no roads in the Big Woods. Can you remember two other things that the Big Woods did *not* have?
Student: *There were no houses. There were no people.*

Instructor: Who *did* live among the trees?
Student: *Wild animals lived among the trees.*

Ask, "What is one thing you remember about the passage?" If the student answers in a fragment, follow the same procedure as above. Write the student's answer down on Student Page 2 as he watches. (This answer can be the same as one of the answers above.) Point out the capital letter that begins the sentence and the period that ends it.

DAY THREE: Copywork   *Student Page 3*

Focus: *Beginning capitals and ending periods*

Pull out Student Page 3. Write the student's name and the date for him as he watches, or ask him to write the name and date independently. The following two model sentences are already printed on it:

> Pa owned a pig.
> There was plenty of fresh meat to last for a long time.

Ask the student to look carefully at the sentences. While he is examining the sentences, explain that these sentences are also from *Little House in the Big Woods*. Ask the student to point out the capital letters that begin the sentences, and the periods that end them. Tell him that both of these are **complete sentences**.

Choose whichever sentence is appropriate to the student's handwriting ability and ask the student to copy it on the lines provided. Watch the student as he writes in pencil. If he begins to make an error, gently stop him and ask him to look at the model again.

DAY FOUR: Narration Exercise   *Student Page 4*

Pull out Student Page 4. Write the student's name and the date for him as he watches, or ask him to write the name and date independently.

Read the following passage out loud to the student. Before you begin, explain that the Ingalls family needed the pig so that they would have meat to eat in the winter; since there were no grocery stores, Pa had to raise the pig for food.

> Once in the middle of the night Laura woke up and heard the pig squealing. Pa jumped out of bed, snatched his gun from the wall, and ran outdoors. Then Laura heard the gun go off once, twice.
>
> When Pa came back, he told what had happened. He had seen a big black bear standing beside the pigpen. The bear was reaching into the pen to grab the pig, and the pig was running and squealing. Pa saw this in the starlight and he fired quickly. But the light was dim and in his haste he missed the bear. The bear ran away into the woods, not hurt at all.
>
> —From *Little House in the Big Woods*
> by Laura Ingalls Wilder

Ask the following questions, following the instructions in Day Two:

Instructor: What did Laura hear when she woke up?
Student: *She heard the pig squealing.*

Instructor: What did Pa do when he heard the pig squeal?
Student: *He got his gun and went outside.*

Instructor: How many times did the gun go off?
Student: *It went off twice.*

Instructor: What did Pa see when he went outside?
Student: *He saw a black bear standing beside the pigpen.*

Instructor: What was the bear trying to do?
Student: *It was trying to grab the pig.*

Instructor: When Pa shot at the bear, he missed because he was in a hurry. What is the other reason that he missed the bear?
Student: *The light was dim.*

Ask, "What is one thing you remember about the passage?" Help the student to form a complete sentence if necessary. Write the student's answer down on Student Page 4 as he watches. This answer can be the same as one of the answers above.

WEEK 2

DAY ONE: Copywork   *Student Page 5*

Focus: *Capitalizing first (proper) names*

Pull out Student Page 5. Write the student's name and the date for her as she watches, or ask her to write the name and date independently. The following two model sentences are already printed on it:

> Geppetto made Pinocchio.
> Geppetto decided to make a wooden puppet named Pinocchio.

Ask the student to look carefully at the sentences. Explain that these sentences are from *The Adventures of Pinocchio,* by Carlo Collodi. *The Adventures of Pinocchio* is a story about a wooden puppet and his poor carpenter father, Geppetto. Ask the student to point out the first names in the sentences, and then the capital letters that begin each first name. Remind her that all first names are **proper nouns**, and are capitalized.

Watch the student as she writes in pencil. If she begins to make an error, gently stop her and ask her to look at the model again.

DAY TWO: Narration Exercise   *Student Page 6*

Pull out Student Page 6. Write the student's name and the date for her as she watches, or ask her to write the name and date independently.

Read the following passage from *The Adventures of Pinocchio* out loud to the student. Explain that the carpenter Geppetto has found a beautiful piece of wood, and has decided to make a marionette (a puppet which is worked by strings that the puppetmaster holds from above).

> Little as Geppetto's house was, it was neat and comfortable. It was a small room on the ground floor, with a tiny window under the stairway.
>
> The furniture could not have been much simpler: a very old chair, a rickety old bed, and a tumble-down table. A fireplace full of burning logs was painted on the wall opposite the door. Over the fire, there was painted a pot full of something which kept boiling happily away and sending up clouds of what looked like real steam.
>
> As soon as he reached home, Geppetto took his tools and began to cut and shape the wood into a marionette.
>
> "What shall I call him?" he said to himself. "I think I'll call him Pinocchio."
>
> —From *The Adventures of Pinocchio*
> By Carlo Collodi

Ask the following questions. Remind the student to answer you in complete sentences. If she answers in a fragment, turn the fragment into a complete sentence, say it to her, and then ask her to repeat this sentence back to you. If she cannot answer a question, read her the part of the passage that contains the answer, and then ask the question again.

Instructor: Was Geppetto's house big or small?
Student: *It was small.*

Instructor: Was it messy?
Student: *No, it was neat.* [If the student simply answers "No," ask, "What was it like?"]

Instructor: Geppetto had furniture in his room. Can you remember two of the pieces of furniture that were in his room?
Student: *He had a chair, a bed, and a table.*

Instructor: What was painted on one of the walls in his room?
Student: *A fireplace was painted on the wall.*

Instructor: What was painted above the fire?
Student: *A pot sending out steam was painted over the fire.*

Instructor: What did Geppetto begin to make when he got home?
Student: *Gepetto began to make a puppet OR a marionette.*

Instructor: Geppetto decided to name the marionette. What name did he give him?
Student: *Geppetto named him Pinocchio.*

Ask, "What is one thing you remember about the passage?" Write the student's answer down on Student Page 6 as she watches. This answer can be the same as one of the answers above.

DAY THREE: Copywork

Student Page 7

Focus: *Beginning capitals and ending periods; capitalizing first (proper) names*

Pull out Student Page 7. Write the student's name and the date for her as she watches, or ask her to write the name and date independently. The following two model sentences are already printed on it:

The puppet was Pinocchio.
Geppetto made the puppet Pinocchio out of wood.

Ask the student to look carefully at the sentences, and to point out the capital letters at the beginning of the sentences and the periods at the end. Then ask her to point out the first names in each sentences. Remind her that all first names are **proper nouns,** and are capitalized. Then, ask her to point out the capital letters that begin each proper noun.

Watch the student as she writes in pencil. If she begins to make an error, gently stop her and ask her to look at the model again.

DAY FOUR: Narration Exercise

Pull out Student Page 8. Write the student's name and the date for her as she watches, or ask her to write the name and date independently.

Read the following passage out loud to the student. Before you begin, explain that Pinocchio has been left alone in the house with nothing to eat.

> For, as night came on, a queer, empty feeling at the pit of his stomach reminded the marionette that he had eaten nothing as yet.
>
> A boy's appetite grows very fast, and in a few moments the queer, empty feeling had become hunger, and the hunger grew bigger and bigger, until soon he was as ravenous as a bear.
>
> Poor Pinocchio ran to the fireplace where the pot was boiling and stretched out his hand to take the cover off, but to his amazement the pot was only painted! Think how he felt! His long nose became at least two inches longer.
>
> He ran about the room, dug in all the boxes and drawers, and even looked under the bed in search of a piece of bread, hard though it might be, or a cookie, or perhaps a bit of fish. A bone left by a dog would have tasted good to him! But he found nothing.
>
> And meanwhile his hunger grew and grew. The only relief poor Pinocchio had was to yawn; and he certainly did yawn, such a big yawn that his mouth stretched out to the tips of his ears. Soon he became dizzy and faint. He wept and wailed to himself: "The Talking Cricket was right. It was wrong of me to disobey Father and to run away from home. If he were here now, I wouldn't be so hungry! Oh, how horrible it is to be hungry!"
>
> Suddenly, he saw, among the sweepings in a corner, something round and white that looked very much like a hen's egg. In a jiffy he pounced upon it. It was an egg.

—From *The Adventures of Pinocchio*
By Carlo Collodi

Ask the following questions:

Instructor: What problem did Pinocchio have at the beginning of the story?
Student: *He was hungry.*

Instructor: What animal was he as hungry as?
Student: *He was as hungry as a bear.*

Instructor: Where did he first go to get some food?
Student: *He ran to the fireplace where the pot was boiling.*

Instructor: Why was he disappointed when he got there?
Student: *He was disappointed because the pot was painted on the wall.*

Instructor: Pinocchio ran around the room looking for food. Can you remember two of the four things he hoped to find?
Student: *He was hoping to find a piece of bread, a cookie, a bit of fish, or a bone left by a dog.*

Instructor: What did Pinocchio finally find in the corner of the room?
Student: *He found an egg.*

Ask, "What is one thing you remember about the passage?" Write the student's answer down on Student Page 8 as she watches. This answer can be the same as one of the answers above.

WEEK 3

DAY ONE: Copywork   *Student Page 9*

Focus: *Beginning capitals and ending periods*

Pull out Student Page 9. Write the student's name and the date for him as he watches, or ask him to write the name and date independently. The following two model sentences are already printed on it:

> A poor miller had a daughter.
> Once upon a time a poor miller had a beautiful daughter.

Ask the student to look carefully at the sentences. Explain that these sentences are from the beginning of the fairy tale called *Rumpelstiltzkin.* You will read more of this story in the next lesson. Ask the student to point out the capital letters and the periods. Tell him that both of these are **complete sentences.**
Choose whichever sentence is appropriate to the student's handwriting ability and ask him to copy it on the lines provided. Watch the student as he writes in pencil. If he begins to make an error, gently stop him and ask him to look at the model again.

DAY TWO: Narration Exercise   *Student Page 10*

Pull out Student Page 10. Write the student's name and the date for him as he watches, or ask him to write the name and date independently.
Read the following passage out loud to the student. Before you begin, explain that this is the beginning of a very old story called *Rumpelstiltzkin.* This version of the story was written down by a man named Andrew Lang in 1889—more than a hundred years ago. Andrew Lang's book contained many old stories which he had collected. It was called *The Blue Fairy Book.*

There was once upon a time a poor miller who had a very beautiful daughter. Now it happened one day that he had an audience with the king, and in order to appear a person of some importance he told him that he had a daughter who could spin straw into gold.

"Now that's a talent worth having," said the king to the miller. "If your daughter is as clever as you say, bring her to my palace to-morrow, and I'll put her to the test."

When the girl was brought to him he led her into a room full of straw, gave her a spinning-wheel and spindle, and said: "Now set to work and spin all night till early dawn, and if by that time you haven't spun the straw into gold you shall die." Then he closed the door behind him and left her alone inside.

So the poor miller's daughter sat down, and didn't know what in the world she was to do. She hadn't the least idea of how to spin straw into gold, and became at last so miserable that she began to cry.

Suddenly the door opened, and in stepped a tiny little man and said: "Good-evening, Miss Miller-maid; why are you crying so bitterly?"

—From *The Blue Fairy Book*
by Andrew Lang

Ask the following questions. Remind the student to answer you in complete sentences. If he answers in a fragment, turn the fragment into a complete sentence, say it to him, and then ask him to repeat this sentence back to you. If he cannot answer a question, read him the part of the passage that contains the answer, and then ask the question again.

Instructor: What did the miller tell the king about his daughter?
Student: *He said that his daughter could spin straw into gold.*

Instructor: Was this true?
Student: *No, it was a lie.* [If necessary, prompt the child for a complete sentence; do not allow him to simply say "No."]

Instructor: Why did the miller tell this lie?
Student: *He wanted to look important.* [You may need to read the first paragraph again to the child before he answers.]

Instructor: When the king heard this, what did he tell the miller to do?
Student: *He told the miller to bring her to the palace.*

Instructor: When the girl came to the palace, where did the king put her?
Student: *He put her in a room full of straw.*

Instructor: What was the girl supposed to do?
Student: *She was supposed to spin the straw into gold.*

Instructor: What happened right at the end of the passage?
Student: *A tiny man came into the room and asked her why she was crying.*

Ask, "What is one thing you remember about the passage?" Write the student's answer down on Student Page 10 as he watches. This answer can be the same as one of the answers above.

DAY THREE: Copywork   *Student Page 11*

Focus: Beginning capitals and ending periods; capitalizing first (proper) names

Pull out Student Page 11. Write the student's name and the date for him as he watches, or ask him to write the name and date independently. The following two model sentences are already printed on it:

> His name was Rumpelstiltzkin.
> She asked him if his name was Sheepshanks or Cruickshanks.

Ask the student to look carefully at the sentences. Tell him that these sentences also come from *Rumpelstiltzkin.* After the tiny man asked the miller's daughter why she was crying, he told her that he would turn the straw into gold as long as she gave him her first baby. She agreed that she would. The little man turned the straw to gold—and the king was so delighted that he married the miller's daughter. When her first baby was born, the tiny man appeared and tried to take it. She begged him to let her keep the baby, and the man told her that she could keep the baby only if she could guess his name.

Ask the student to point out the capital letters that begin both sentences, and the periods that end them. Tell him that both of these are **complete sentences.** Then ask him to point to the first name[s] in each. Remind him that each name is a **proper noun** and begins with a capital letter.

Choose whichever sentence is appropriate to the student's handwriting ability. Watch the student as he writes in pencil. If he begins to make an error, gently stop him and ask him to look at the model again.

DAY FOUR: Narration Exercise   *Student Page 12*

Pull out Student Page 12. Write the student's name and the date for him as he watches, or ask him to write the name and date independently.

Read the following passage from *Rumpelstiltzkin* out loud to the student. Be sure to use slightly different voices for the Queen, the messenger, and Rumpelstiltzkin so that the student can differentiate between the lines of dialogue.

> Then the Queen pondered the whole night over all the names she had ever heard, and sent a messenger to scour the land, and to pick up far and near any names he could come across. When the little man arrived on the following day she began with Kasper, Melchior, Belshazzar, and all the other

names she knew, in a string, but at each one the manikin called out: "That's not my name."

The next day she sent to inquire the names of all the people in the neighborhood, and had a long list of the most uncommon and extraordinary for the little man when he made his appearance. "Is your name, perhaps, Sheepshanks, Cruickshanks, Spindleshanks?" but he always replied: "That's not my name."

On the third day the messenger returned and announced: "I have not been able to find any new names, but as I came upon a high hill round the corner of the wood, where the foxes and hares bid each other good-night, I saw a little house, and in front of the house burned a fire, and round the fire sprang the most grotesque little man, hopping on one leg and crying:

> "To-morrow I brew, to-day I bake,
> And then the child away I'll take;
> For little deems my royal dame
> That Rumpelstiltzkin is my name!"

You can imagine the Queen's delight at hearing the name, and when the little man stepped in shortly afterward and asked: "Now, my lady Queen, what's my name?" she asked first: "Is your name Conrad?"

"NO."

"Is your name Harry?"

"No."

"Is your name perhaps, Rumpelstiltzkin?"

—From *The Blue Fairy Book*
by Andrew Lang

Ask the following questions. Remind the student to answer you in complete sentences. If he answers in a fragment, turn the fragment into a complete sentence, say it to him, and then ask him to repeat this sentence back to you. If he cannot answer a question, read him the part of the passage that contains the answer, and then ask the question again.

Instructor: Whom did the Queen send to find names?
Student: *She sent a messenger.*

Instructor: Can you remember one of the three names that she guessed when the little man first returned?
Student: *She guessed Kasper, Melchior, and Belshazzar.*

Instructor: Where did she look for names next?
Student: *She looked in the neighborhood.*

Instructor: Can you remember one of the three names that she guessed when the little man returned a second time?
Student: *She guessed Sheepshanks, Cruickshanks, and Spindleshanks.*

Instructor: How many days was the messenger gone?
Student: *He was gone three days.*

Instructor: What was Rumpelstiltzkin doing when the messenger saw him?
Student: *He was hopping around a fire.*

Instructor: Can you remember one of the two incorrect names that the queen guessed when Rumpelstiltzkin returned the third time?
Student: *She guessed Conrad and Harry.*

Ask, "What is one thing you remember about the passage?" Write the student's answer down on Student Page 12 as he watches. This answer can be the same as one of the answers above.

WEEK 4

DAY ONE: Copywork   *Student Page 13*

Focus: Beginning capitals and ending periods; capitalizing first (proper) names

Pull out Student Page 13. Write the student's name and the date for her as she watches, or ask her to write the name and date independently. The following two model sentences are already printed on it:

> Alice was silent.
> The caterpillar was the first to speak.

Ask the student to look carefully at the sentences. While she is examining the sentences, explain that these sentences are from *Alice's Adventures in Wonderland*, by Lewis Carroll. Alice has fallen down a rabbit-hole, and now she is wandering through a very strange country. In this country, she is only three inches tall—and she has just met a large blue caterpillar who is sitting on top of a mushroom.

Ask the student to point out the first name in the first sentence. Remind her that names are always capitalized, because they are **proper nouns**. Ask her to point out the capital letter at the beginning of the second sentence and the periods at the end of both sentences.

Watch the student as she writes in pencil. If she begins to make an error, gently stop her and ask her to look at the model again.

DAY TWO: Narration Exercise   *Student Page 14*

Pull out Student Page 14. Write the student's name and the date for her as she watches, or ask her to write the name and date independently.

Explain to the student that a "hookah" is an old-fashioned type of pipe, and that to "contradict" someone is to say the opposite of what they tell you.

The Caterpillar was the first to speak.

"What size do you want to be?" it asked.

"Oh, I'm not particular as to size," Alice hastily replied; "Only one doesn't like changing so often, you know."

"I *don't* know," said the Caterpillar.

Alice said nothing: she had never been so much contradicted in all her life before, and she felt that she was losing her temper.

"Are you content now?" said the Caterpillar.

"Well, I should like to be a *little* larger, sir, if you wouldn't mind," said Alice: "three inches is such a wretched height to be."

"It is a very good height indeed!" said the Caterpillar angrily, rearing itself upright as it spoke (it was exactly three inches high).

"But I'm not used to it!" pleaded poor Alice in a piteous tone. And she thought to herself, "I wish the creatures wouldn't be so easily offended!"

"You'll get used to it in time," said the Caterpillar; and it put the hookah into its mouth and began smoking again.

This time Alice waited patiently until it chose to speak again. In a minute or two the Caterpillar took the hookah out of its mouth and yawned once or twice, and shook itself. Then it got down off the mushroom, and crawled away into the grass merely remarking as it went, "One side will make you grow taller, and the other side will make you grow shorter."

"One side of *what?* The other side of *what?*" thought Alice to herself.

"Of the mushroom," said the Caterpillar, just as if she had asked it aloud; and in another moment it was out of sight.

—From *Alice's Adventures in Wonderland*
by Lewis Carroll

Ask the following questions. Remind the student to answer you in complete sentences. If she answers in a fragment, turn the fragment into a complete sentence, say it to her, and then ask her to repeat this sentence back to you. If she cannot answer a question, read her the part of the passage that contains the answer, and then ask the question again.

Instructor: How tall is the Caterpillar?
Student: He is three inches tall.

Instructor: Does Alice like being three inches tall?
Student: No, she doesn't.

Instructor: Does she want to be smaller or larger?
Student: She wants to be larger.

Instructor: What does the Caterpillar tell Alice, right before he crawls away?
Student: He says, "One side will make you taller and the other will make you shorter."

Instructor: What is he talking about?
Student: He is talking about the mushroom.

Ask, "What is one thing you remember about the passage?" Write the student's answer down on Student Page 14 as she watches. This answer can be the same as one of the answers above.

DAY THREE: Copywork   *Student Page 15*

Focus: *Beginning capitals and ending periods; capitalizing first (proper) names*

Pull out Student Page 15. Write the student's name and the date for her as she watches, or ask her to write the name and date independently. The following two model sentences are already printed on it:

> The first witness was the Hatter.
> One of the jurors had a pencil that squeaked.

Ask the student to look carefully at the sentences. Explain that, at the end of *Alice's Adventures in Wonderland,* Alice goes to the trial of the Knave of Hearts, who is accused of stealing a plate of tarts (which are like tiny pies) from the Queen of Hearts. There are twelve "jurors" at the trial—animals who will listen to the evidence and decide whether the Knave of Hearts is guilty.

Ask the student to point out the beginning capitals and ending periods. Explain that "Hatter" begins with a capital letter because the writer Lewis Carroll is using it as a first (proper) name.

Choose whichever sentence is appropriate to the student's handwriting ability. Watch the student as she writes in pencil. If she begins to make an error, gently stop her and ask her to look at the model again.

DAY FOUR: Narration Exercise and Copywork   *Student Page 16*

Pull out Student Page 16. Write the student's name and the date for her as she watches, or ask her to write the name and date independently.

Read the following passage about the trial in *Alice's Adventures in Wonderland* out loud to the student.

> The King and Queen of Hearts were seated on their throne when they arrived, with a great crowd assembled about them—all sorts of little birds and beasts, as well as the whole pack of cards: the Knave was standing before them, in chains, with a soldier on each side to guard him; and near the King was the White Rabbit, with a trumpet in one hand, and a scroll of parchment in the other. In the very middle of the court was a table, with a large dish of tarts upon it: they looked so good, that it made Alice quite hungry to look at them—"I wish they'd get the trial done," she thought, "and

hand round the refreshments!" But there seemed to be no chance of this, so she began looking about her, to pass away the time.

Alice had never been in a court of justice before, but she had read about them in books, and she was quite pleased to find that she knew the name of nearly everything there. "That's the judge," she said to herself, "because of his great wig." The judge, by the way, was the King; and as he wore his crown over the wig...he did not look at all comfortable, and it was certainly not becoming.

"And that's the jury-box," thought Alice, "and those twelve creatures" (she was obliged to say "creatures," you see, because some of them were animals, and some were birds), "I suppose they are the jurors." She said this last word two or three times over to herself, being rather proud of it: for she thought, and rightly too, that very few little girls of her age knew the meaning of it at all. However, "jurymen" would have done just as well.

—From *Alice's Adventures in Wonderland*
by Lewis Carroll

Ask the following questions. Remind the student to answer you in complete sentences. If she answers in a fragment, turn the fragment into a complete sentence, say it to her, and then ask her to repeat this sentence back to you. If she cannot answer a question, read her the part of the passage that contains the answer, and then ask the question again.

Instructor: Besides Alice, can you name two other characters who were in the part of the story I just read?
Student: *The King and Queen of Hearts, the Knave of Hearts, and the White Rabbit were all in the story.*

Instructor: What was on the table in the very middle of the court?
Student: *There was a large dish of tarts on the table.*

Instructor: What was the judge wearing that helped Alice recognize him?
Student: *He was wearing a wig.*

Instructor: Who was the judge?
Student: *The judge was the King of Hearts.*

Instructor: Who were the jurors?
Student: *The jurors were animals and birds.*

Instructor: Why was Alice proud of knowing the word "juror"?
Student: *She thought that few little girls her age would know that word.*

Ask, "What is one thing you remember about the passage?" Write the student's answer down on the "Instructor" lines of Student Page 16 as she watches. This answer can be the same as one of the answers above.

Now ask the student to copy the sentence in pencil on the "Student" lines below the model. If the sentence is too long for comfort, she can copy only the first six to eight words.

WEEK 5

DAY ONE: Copywork   *Student Page 17*

Focus: *Capitalizing first and last names*

Pull out Student Page 17. Write the student's name and the date for him as he watches, or ask him to write the name and date independently. The following two model sentences are already printed on it:

> Jacob Grimm wrote down fairy tales.
> Jacob Grimm and Wilhelm Grimm were brothers who
>   collected fairy tales.

Ask the student to look carefully at the sentences. While he is examining the sentences, explain that Jacob and Wilhelm Grimm lived in Germany over a hundred years ago. They collected fairy tales that the German people had been telling each other for many years and wrote them down. Many of the stories that children know come from the books written by the Grimm brothers.

Remind the student that both the first and last names of people are **proper nouns**. Ask the student to point out which of these names are first names and which are last names. Jacob and Wilhelm Grimm have the same last name, or family name, because they are brothers. Now ask the student to point out the capital letters that begin the first and last names.

Choose whichever sentence is appropriate to the student's handwriting ability and ask the student to copy it. Watch the student as he writes in pencil. If he begins to make an error, gently stop him and ask him to look at the model again.

DAY TWO: Narration Exercise   *Student Page 18*

Pull out Student Page 18. Write the student's name and the date for him as he watches, or ask him to write the name and date independently.

Tell the student that the following story is from the beginning of one of the Grimms' fairy tales.

> One fine evening a young princess went out to take a walk by herself in a wood. When she came to a cool spring of water, she sat herself down to rest a while.
>
> Now she had a golden ball in her hand, which was her favourite plaything; and she was always tossing it up into the air, and catching it again as it fell. After a time she threw it up so high that she missed catching it as it fell; and the ball bounded away, and rolled along upon the ground, till at last it fell down into the spring. The princess looked into the spring after her ball, but it was very deep, so deep that she could not see the bottom of it. Then she began to wail over her loss, and said, "Alas! if I could only get my ball

again, I would give all my fine clothes and jewels, and everything that I have in the world."

While she was speaking, a frog put its head out of the water, and said, "Princess, why do you weep so bitterly?"

"Alas!" said she, "what can you do for me, you nasty frog? My golden ball has fallen into the spring."

The frog said, "I don't want your pearls, and jewels, and fine clothes; but if you will love me, and let me live with you and eat from off your golden plate, and sleep upon your bed, I will bring you your ball again."

The princess thought to herself, "What nonsense this silly frog is talking! He can never even get out of the spring to visit me, so I will agree." So she said to the frog, "Well, if you will bring me my ball, I will do all you ask."

Then the frog put his head down, and dove deep under the water. After a little while he came up again, with the ball in his mouth, and threw it on the edge of the spring. As soon as the young princess saw her ball, she ran to pick it up; and she was so overjoyed to have it in her hand again, that she never thought of the frog, but ran home with it as fast as she could.

The frog called after her, "Stay, princess, and take me with you as you said." But she did not stop to hear a word.

—From "The Frog Prince," by Jacob and Wilhelm Grimm
translated by Edgar Taylor and Marian Edwardes,
slightly condensed and modernized by Susan Wise Bauer

Ask the following questions. Remind the student to answer you in complete sentences. If he answers in a fragment, turn the fragment into a complete sentence, say it to him, and then ask him to repeat this sentence back to you. If he cannot answer a question, read him the part of the passage that contains the answer, and then ask the question again.

Instructor: What did the princess have in her hand?
Student: *She had a golden ball.*

Instructor: What happened to the golden ball?
Student: *It fell into the water OR She was throwing it up and down, and it fell into the spring.*

Instructor: What came out of the water to ask her why she was crying?
Student: *A frog came out of the water.*

Instructor: The frog asked for four things, in return for getting the ball back. Can you remember two of them?
Student: *He wanted the princess to love him; he wanted to live with her; he wanted to eat off her golden plate; he wanted to sleep on her bed.*

Instructor: Why did the princess agree to this?
Student: *She thought that the frog couldn't get out of the spring.*

Instructor: When the princess had her ball back, what did she do?
Student: *She ran home without listening to the frog.*

Instructor: What did the frog do when the princess ran home?
Student: *He called after her.*

Ask, "What is one thing you remember about the passage?" Write the student's answer down on Student Page 18 as he watches. This answer can be the same as one of the answers above.

DAY THREE: Copywork   *Student Page 19*

Focus: *Capitalizing first and last names*

Pull out Student Page 19. Write the student's name and the date for him as he watches, or ask him to write the name and date independently. The following two model sentences are already printed on it:

> Edgar Taylor translated the fairy tales.
> Edgar Taylor and Marian Edwardes translated the fairy tales
>   into English.

Ask the student to look carefully at the sentences. While he is examining the sentences, tell him that Jacob and Wilhelm Grimm lived in Germany. The Grimm brothers first published their fairy tales in 1812, almost two hundred years ago. About ten years later, in 1823, two English writers named Edgar Taylor and Marian Edwardes translated the German stories into English so that English-speaking children could read them. Ask the student to point out the capital letters that begin the first and last names in the sentences.

Choose whichever sentence is appropriate to the student's handwriting ability. Watch the student as he writes in pencil. If he begins to make an error, gently stop him and ask him to look at the model again.

DAY FOUR: Narration Exercise and Copywork   *Student Page 20*

Pull out Student Page 20. Write the student's name and the date for him as he watches, or ask him to write the name and date independently.

Tell the student that, in the fairy tale, the princess went home and ate dinner with her father, the king. While she was eating, the frog came to the door of the palace and begged for the princess to fulfill her promise. The king listened to the frog's story. Here is what he said to his daughter:

Then the king said to the young princess, "As you have given your word you must keep it; so go and let him in."

She did so, and the frog hopped into the room, and then straight on—tap, tap, plash, plash—From the bottom of the room to the top, till he came up close to the table where the princess sat.

"Please, lift me up on your chair," he said to the princess, "and let me sit next to you." As soon as she had done this, the frog said, "Put your plate nearer to me, that I may eat out of it." This she did, and when he had eaten as much as he could, he said, "Now I am tired; carry me upstairs, and put me into your bed."

And the princess, though very unwilling, took him up in her hand, and put him upon the pillow of her own bed, where he slept all night long.

As soon as it was light he jumped up, hopped downstairs, and went out of the house. "Now, then," thought the princess, "at last he is gone, and I shall be troubled with him no more."

But she was mistaken; for when night came again she heard the same tapping at the door. When the princess opened the door the frog came in, and slept upon her pillow as before, till the morning broke. And the third night he did the same.

But when the princess awoke on the following morning she was astonished to see, instead of the frog, a handsome prince standing at the head of her bed.

He told her that he had been enchanted by a spiteful fairy, who had changed him into a frog; and that he had been cursed to remain a frog until a princess should take him out of the spring, and let him eat from her plate, and sleep upon her bed for three nights. "You," said the prince, "have broken the spell. Please, come with me to my father's kingdom, where I will marry you, and love you as long as you live."

—From "The Frog Prince," by Jacob and Wilhelm Grimm
translated by Edgar Taylor and Marian Edwardes,
slightly condensed and modernized by Susan Wise Bauer

Ask the following questions. Remind the student to answer you in complete sentences. If he answers in a fragment, turn the fragment into a complete sentence, say it to him, and then ask him to repeat this sentence back to you. If he cannot answer a question, read him the part of the passage that contains the answer, and then ask the question again.

Instructor: What did the king tell his daughter?
Student: *He told her that she had to keep her promise.*

Instructor: Where did the frog insist on sitting?
Student: *He wanted to sit on the princess's chair.*

Instructor: What did the frog eat out of?
Student: *He ate out of the princess's plate.*

Instructor: Where did he insist on sleeping?
Student: He slept on the princess's bed.

Instructor: When the frog hopped out of the princess's room in the morning, what did she think?
Student: She thought that he was gone.

Instructor: Was the frog gone for good?
Student: No; he came back.

Instructor: How many nights did the frog stay with the princess?
Student: He stayed for three nights.

Instructor: What did he change into on the third day?
Student: He changed into a handsome prince.

Ask, "What is one thing you remember about the passage?" Write the student's answer down on the "Instructor" lines of Student Page 20 as he watches. This answer can be the same as one of the answers above.

Now ask the student to copy the sentence in pencil on the "Student" lines below the model. If the sentence is too long for comfort, he can copy only the first six to eight words.

WEEK 6

DAY ONE: Copywork   *Student Page 21*

Focus: *Capitalizing first and last names; forming commas*

Pull out Student Page 21. Write the student's name and the date for her as she watches, or ask her to write the name and date independently.

The following two model sentences are already printed on the Student Page:

Jane and Michael Banks stared.
Jane and Michael Banks stared at their new nanny, Mary Poppins.

Ask the student to look carefully at the sentences. Explain that the book *Mary Poppins* is the first in a series of stories about a mysterious and magical English nanny named Mary Poppins. She comes to live with the Banks family in London to take care of the children.

Remind the student that first and last names are **proper nouns**. Ask the student to point out the capital letters that begin the first and last names in both sentences. Remind her that names are always capitalized because they are proper nouns.

Point out the comma in the second sentence. Ask the student to practice making commas in the blank space at the bottom of Student Page 21. Commas are like periods with little tails that curve off to the left.

Choose whichever sentence is appropriate to the student's handwriting ability. Watch the student as she writes in pencil. If she begins to make an error, gently stop her and ask her to look at the model again.

DAY TWO: Narration Exercise   *Student Page 22*

Pull out Student Page 22. Write the student's name and the date for her as she watches, or ask her to write the name and date independently.

Read the following passage out loud to the student. Explain that Mary Poppins has just arrived and taken the position as the nanny for the Banks children: Jane, Michael, and the baby twins, who are named John and Barbara. In this part of the story, Mary Poppins is opening her large bag as Jane and Michael look on.

You may need to explain that "lozenges" are small hard candies that have medicine in them.

> By this time the bag was open, and Jane and Michael were more than surprised to find it was completely empty.
>
> "Why," said Jane, "there's nothing in it!"
>
> "What do you mean—nothing?" demanded Mary Poppins, drawing herself up and looking as though she had been insulted. "Nothing in it, did you say?"
>
> And with that she took out from the empty bag a starched white apron and tied it round her waist. Next she unpacked a large cake of Sunlight soap, a toothbrush, a packet of hairpins, a bottle of scent, a small folding armchair and a box of lozenges.
>
> Jane and Michael stared.
>
> "But I saw," whispered Michael. "It was empty."
>
> "Hush!" said Jane, as Mary Poppins took out a large bottle labelled "One Tea-Spoon to be Taken at Bed-Time."
>
> A spoon was attached to the neck of the bottle, and into this Mary Poppins poured a dark crimson fluid.
>
> "Is that your medicine?" enquired Michael, looking very interested.
>
> "No, yours," said Mary Poppins, holding out the spoon to him. Michael stared. He wrinkled up his nose. He began to protest.
>
> "I don't want it. I don't need it. I won't!"
>
> But Mary Poppins's eyes were fixed upon him, and Michael suddenly discovered that you could not look at Mary Poppins and disobey her.

—From *Mary Poppins*
by P. L. Travers

Ask the following questions. Remind the student to answer you in complete sentences. If she answers in a fragment, turn the fragment into a complete sentence, say it to her, and then ask her to repeat this sentence back to you. If she cannot answer a question, read her the part of the passage that contains the answer, and then ask the question again.

Instructor: What did Jane and Michael see when they looked into Mary Poppins's bag?
Student: *They didn't see anything in it.*

Instructor: What is the first thing that Mary Poppins pulled out of her bag?
Student: *She pulled out a white apron.*

Instructor: Mary Poppins then pulled several other items out of her bag. Can you remember two of them?
Student: *She pulled out soap, a toothbrush, hairpins, a bottle of scent, a small folding armchair, and a box of lozenges.*

Instructor: What did Mary Poppins pull out of the bag to give to Michael?
Student: *She pulled out some medicine.*

Instructor: What color was the medicine?
Student: *It was dark crimson OR dark red.*

Instructor: What did Michael do when he learned that the medicine was for him?
Student: *He said that he didn't want it.*

Instructor: Was Michael able to disobey Mary Poppins?
Student: *No, he was not.*

Ask, "What is one thing you remember about the passage?" Write the student's answer down on Student Page 22 as she watches. This answer can be the same as one of the answers above.

DAY THREE: Copywork   *Student Page 23*

Focus: *Capitalizing first and last names; forming commas*

Pull out Student Page 23. Write the student's name and the date for her as she watches, or ask her to write the name and date independently.

The following two model sentences are already printed on the Student Page:

> Mary Poppins gave Jane and Michael medicine.
> Mary Poppins taught Jane and Michael Banks how to say the word
>   supercalifragilisticexpialidocius.

Ask the student to look carefully at the sentences. Explain that Mary Poppins is the full name of Jane and Michael's new nanny. Remind the student that both first and last names are capitalized. Jane and Michael are the first names of the older Banks children; Banks is their last name. Sound out the word *"supercalifragilisticexpialidocius"* for the student and explain that this a nonsense word, made up for fun.

Ask the student to practice making commas at the bottom of Student Page 23.

Choose whichever sentence is appropriate to the student's handwriting ability and ask her to copy it on the lines provided. Watch the student as she writes in pencil. If she begins to make an error, gently stop her and ask her to look at the model again.

DAY FOUR: Narration Exercise and Copywork   *Student Page 24*

Pull out Student Page 24. Write the student's name and the date for her as she watches, or ask her to write the name and date independently.

Explain to the student that the following passage from *Mary Poppins* describes the magic medicine that she gives the children. It changes its taste every time a new person swallows it. John and Barbara are the baby twins in the Banks family; Michael is the first child to take the medicine.

There was something strange and extraordinary about her—something that was frightening and at the same time most exciting. The spoon came nearer. He held his breath, shut his eyes and gulped. A delicious taste ran round his mouth. He turned his tongue in it. He swallowed, and a happy smile ran round his face.

"Strawberry ice," he said ecstatically. "More, more, more!"

But Mary Poppins, her face as stern as before, was pouring out a dose for Jane. It ran into the spoon, silvery, greeny, yellowy. Jane tasted it.

"Lime-juice cordial," she said, sliding her tongue deliciously over her lips. But when she saw Mary Poppins moving towards the twins with the bottle, Jane rushed at her.

"Oh no—please. They're too young. It wouldn't be good for them. Please!"

Mary Poppins, however, took no notice, but with a warning, terrible glance at Jane, tipped the spoon towards John's mouth. He lapped at it eagerly, and by the few drops that were spilt on his bib, Jane and Michael could tell that the substance in the spoon this time was milk. Then Barbara had her share, and she gurgled and licked the spoon twice.

Mary Poppins then poured out another dose and solemnly took it herself.

"Rum punch," she said, smacking her lips and corking the bottle.

Jane's eyes and Michael's popped with astonishment, but they were not given much time to wonder, for Mary Poppins, having put the miraculous bottle on the mantelpiece, turned to them.

"Now," she said, "spit-spot into bed."

—From *Mary Poppins*
by P. L. Travers

Ask the following questions. Remind the student to answer you in complete sentences. If she answers in a fragment, turn the fragment into a complete sentence, say it to her, and then ask her to repeat this sentence back to you. If she cannot answer a question, read her the part of the passage that contains the answer, and then ask the question again.

Instructor: What did Michael's medicine taste like?
Student: *It tasted like strawberry ice* [ice cream].

Instructor: What fruit did Jane's medicine taste like?
Student: *It tasted like limes.*

Instructor: Why did Jane not want Mary Poppins to give medicine to the twins?
Student: *They were too young.*

Instructor: What did the twins' medicine turn into?
Student: *It turned into milk.*

Instructor: After everyone had their medicine, what did Mary Poppins tell them to do?
Student: *She told them to go to bed.*

Ask, "What is one thing you remember about the passage?" Write down the student's answer on the "Instructor" lines of Student Page 24 as she watches. This answer can be the same as one of the answers above.

Now ask the student to copy the sentence in pencil on the "Student" lines below the model. If the sentence is too long for comfort, she can copy only the first six to eight words.

WEEK 7

DAY ONE: Copywork   *Student Page 25*

Focus: Capitalizing first and last names; forming commas

Pull out Student Page 25. Write the student's name and the date for him as he watches, or ask him to write the name and date independently. The following two model sentences are already printed on it:

> Peter Rabbit lived under a fir tree.
> Flopsy, Mopsy, and Cottontail were good little bunnies.

Ask the student to look carefully at the sentences. While he is examining the sentences, explain that these sentences are from the story *Peter Rabbit,* by Beatrix Potter. Point out that in this story, "Peter Rabbit" is a full, proper name. "Peter" is the first name and "Rabbit" is the last name. Ask the student to point out the capital letters in each of the proper names; then ask him to point out the commas in the second sentence. If necessary, the student can practice writing commas at the bottom of Student Page 25.

Choose whichever sentence is appropriate to the student's handwriting ability. Watch the student as he writes in pencil. If he begins to make an error, gently stop him and ask him to look at the model again.

DAY TWO: Narration Exercise   *Student Page 26*

Pull out Student Page 26. Write the student's name and the date for him as he watches, or ask him to write the name and date independently.

Read the following story to the student. You may need to explain that a "cucumber frame" is a wooden box without a bottom that sits on the ground. The box has a glass top that opens and closes. When the sun shines on the cucumber box, it grows warm like a tiny greenhouse.

> Once upon a time there were four little rabbits, and their names were Flopsy, Mopsy, Cottontail, and Peter.
>
> They lived with their mother in a sand-bank, underneath the root of a very big fir tree.
>
> "Now, my dears," said old Mrs. Rabbit one morning, "you may go into the fields or down the lane, but don't go into Mr. McGregor's garden: your Father had an accident there; he was put in a pie by Mrs. McGregor. Now run along, and don't get into mischief. I am going out."
>
> Then old Mrs. Rabbit took a basket and her umbrella, to the baker's. She bought a loaf of brown bread and five currant buns.
>
> Flopsy, Mopsy, and Cottontail, who were good little bunnies, went down the lane to gather blackberries;
>
> But Peter, who was very naughty, ran straight away to Mr. McGregor's garden and squeezed under the gate!
>
> First he ate some lettuces and some French beans; and then he ate some radishes. And then, feeling rather sick, he went to look for some parsley.
>
> But round the end of a cucumber frame, whom should he meet but Mr. McGregor!
>
> —From *The Tale of Peter Rabbit*
> by Beatrix Potter

Ask the following questions. Remind the student to answer you in complete sentences. If he answers in a fragment, turn the fragment into a complete sentence, say it to him, and then ask him to repeat this sentence back to you. If he cannot answer a question, read him the part of the passage that contains the answer, and then ask the question again.

Instructor: Where did the Rabbit family live?
Student: *They lived in a sand-bank OR They lived underneath the root of a fir tree.*

Instructor: What were the names of the four little rabbits?
Student: *They were named Flopsy, Mopsy, Cottontail, and Peter.*

Instructor: Mrs. Rabbit told the little rabbits two places where they could go. Can you remember one of those places?
Student: *They could go into the fields OR They could go down the lane.*

Instructor: Where did she tell them *not* to go?
Student: *She told them not to go into Mr. McGregor's garden.*

Instructor: Mrs. Rabbit had to go on an errand to the baker's. Can you remember one thing she bought there?
Student: *She bought a loaf of brown bread OR She bought five currant buns.*

Instructor: What did Flopsy, Mopsy, and Cottontail do?
Student: *They went to gather blackberries.*

Instructor: Where did Peter go?
Student: *He went into Mr. McGregor's garden.*

Instructor: Can you remember two things that Peter ate in the garden?
Student: *He ate lettuce, some French beans, radishes, and parsley.*

Instructor: What happened when he went around the end of the cucumber frame?
Student: *He met Mr. McGregor.*

Ask, "What is one thing you remember about the passage?" Write the student's answer down on Student Page 26 as she watches. This answer can be the same as one of the answers above.

DAY THREE: Copywork   *Student Page 27*

Focus: *Capitalizing names of cities and towns; forming commas*

Pull out Student Page 27. Write the student's name and the date for him as he watches, or ask him to write the name and date independently.
The following two model sentences are already printed on it:

> Beatrix Potter was born in London.
> Beatrix Potter was born in London, but she bought a farm in
>   Sawrey, England.

Ask the student to look carefully at the sentences. Tell him to point out the names "London" and "Sawrey". "London" is the name of a city, and "Sawrey" is the name of a town. The names of cities and towns are capitalized, just like the names of people. Have the student point to the capital letter that begins each name. Tell him that "England" is the name of the country where London and Sawrey are located.

Choose whichever sentence is appropriate to the student's handwriting. Watch the student as he writes in pencil. If he copies the second sentence, ask him to point out each comma as he writes. If he begins to make an error, gently stop him and ask him to look at the model again.

Day Four: Narration Exercise and Copywork   *Student Page 28*

Pull out Student Page 28. Write the student's name and the date for him as he watches, or ask him to write the name and date independently.

Read the following passage out loud to the student. You may want to explain that a "sieve" is a large, bowl-shaped strainer with holes in it. A "gooseberry net" is a lightweight net, like a fishnet, laid over berry bushes to keep the birds from eating the berries.

> Mr. McGregor was on his hands and knees planting out young cabbages, but he jumped up and ran after Peter, waving a rake and calling out, "Stop thief!"
>
> Peter was most dreadfully frightened; he rushed all over the garden, for he had forgotten the way back to the gate.
>
> He lost one of his shoes among the cabbages, and the other shoe amongst the potatoes.
>
> After losing them, he ran on four legs and went faster, so that I think he might have got away altogether if he had not unfortunately run into a gooseberry net, and got caught by the large buttons on his jacket. It was a blue jacket with brass buttons, quite new.
>
> Peter gave himself up for lost, and shed big tears; but his sobs were overheard by some friendly sparrows, who flew to him in great excitement, and implored him to exert himself.
>
> Mr. McGregor came up with a sieve, which he intended to pop upon the top of Peter; but Peter wriggled out just in time, leaving his jacket behind him, and rushed into the toolshed, and jumped into a can. It would have been a beautiful thing to hide in, if it had not had so much water in it.
>
> Mr. McGregor was quite sure that Peter was somewhere in the toolshed, perhaps hidden underneath a flower-pot. He began to turn them over carefully looking under each.
>
> Presently Peter sneezed "Kertyschoo!"
>
> Mr. McGregor was after him in no time, and tried to put his foot upon Peter, who jumped out of a window, upsetting three plants.
>
> —From *The Tale of Peter Rabbit*
> by Beatrix Potter

Ask the following questions. Remind the student to answer you in complete sentences. If he answers in a fragment, turn the fragment into a complete sentence, say it to him, and then ask him to repeat this sentence back to you. If he cannot answer a question, read him the part of the passage that contains the answer, and then ask the question again.

Instructor: Peter ran into Mr. McGregor. What did Mr. McGregor call Peter?
Student: *He called Peter a thief.*

Instructor: As Peter was running away, he lost something. What did he lose?
Student: *He lost his shoes—one among the cabbages and another among the potatoes.*

Instructor: What did Peter get caught by, when he ran into the gooseberry net?
Student: *He got caught by the buttons on his jacket.*

Instructor: Who told Peter to keep on trying to escape?
Student: *Friendly sparrows told him to try harder.*

Instructor: Where did Peter next hide from Mr. McGregor?
Student: *He hid in the toolshed OR He hid inside a can that had water in it.*

Instructor: What did Peter do that helped Mr. McGregor find him?
Student: *He sneezed.*

Instructor: How did Peter get away?
Student: *He jumped out of a window.*

Ask, "What is one thing you remember about the passage?" Write the student's answer down on the "Instructor" lines of Student Page 28 as she watches. This answer can be the same as one of the answers above.

Now ask the student to copy the sentence in pencil on the "Student" lines below the model. If the sentence is too long for comfort, he can copy only the first six to eight words.

WEEK 8

Day One: Copywork   *Student Page 29*

Focus: *Capitalizing names of cities and states*

Pull out Student Page 29. Write the student's name and the date for her as she watches, or ask her to write the name and date independently.

The following two model sentences are already printed on the Student Page:

> The Woodlawn family was from Boston.
> Caddie Woodlawn and her family moved to the state of Wisconsin.

Ask the student to look carefully at the sentences. Explain that the book *Caddie Woodlawn* is about a family living in the state of Wisconsin 150 years ago. The main character, Caddie, is an 11-year-old girl who loves to go on adventures with her brothers.

Explain to the student that the names of cities and states are **proper names**, just like the first and last names of people. Ask the student to point out the capital letters that begin the names "Boston" (a city) and "Wisconsin" (a state).

Choose whichever sentence is appropriate to the student's handwriting ability. Watch the student as she writes in pencil. If she begins to make an error, gently stop her and ask her to look at the model again.

DAY TWO: Narration Exercise   *Student Page 30*

Pull out Student Page 30. Write the student's name and the date for her as she watches, or ask her to write the name and date independently.

Explain to the student that Caddie and her brothers have been out all afternoon, picking hazelnuts. Caddie stays out late—even later than her brother Tom. Suddenly she realizes that she may be late for dinner.

You may need to explain that a circuit rider was a pastor who travelled around from church to church on horseback, because many churches were too small to pay a full-time pastor.

> Caddie picked furiously, filling her skirt. It was not often that she got more nuts than Tom. Today she would have more than anybody. An evening stillness crept through the golden woods. Suddenly Caddie knew that she had better go or supper would be begun. To be late for a meal was one of the unpardonable sins in the Woodlawn family. Clutching the edges of her heavy skirt, she began to run. A thorn reached out and tore her sleeve, twigs caught in her tangled hair, her face was dirty and streaked with perspiration, but she didn't stop running until she reached the farmhouse. In fact, she didn't stop even then, for the deserted look of the yard told her that they were all at supper. She rushed on, red and disheveled, and flung open the dining-room door.
>
> There she stopped for the first time, frozen with astonishment and dismay. It wasn't an ordinary supper. It was a company supper! Everybody was calm and clean and sedate, and at one end of the table sat the circuit rider! Paralyzed with horror, Caddie's fingers let go her skirt, and a flood of green hazelnuts rolled all over the floor. In a terrible lull in the conversation they could be heard bumping and rattling to the farthest corners of the room.

—From *Caddie Woodlawn*
by Carol Ryrie Brink

Ask the following questions. Remind the student to answer you in complete sentences. If she answers in a fragment, turn the fragment into a complete sentence, say it to her, and then ask her to repeat this sentence back to you. If she cannot answer a question, read her the part of the passage that contains the answer, and then ask the question again.

Instructor: What was Caddie gathering?
Student: She was picking nuts OR hazelnuts.

Instructor: Why did she stay out so late?
Student: She wanted to get more nuts than anybody.

Instructor: Why did she suddenly decide to go home?
Student: She was afraid she would be late for supper.

Instructor: Did Caddie stop and clean herself up?
Student: No, she ran straight into the dining room.

Instructor: When she opened the door, what did Caddie see?
Student: She saw that this was a company supper.

Instructor: What did Caddie drop on the floor when she opened the door?
Student: She dropped all of her hazelnuts on the floor.

Ask, "What is one thing you remember about the passage?" Write the student's answer down on Student Page 30 as she watches. This answer can be the same as one of the answers above.

Day Three: Copywork   *Student Page 31*

Focus: *Capitalizing names of cities and states*

Pull out Student Page 31. Write the student's name and the date for her as she watches, or ask her to write the name and date independently.

The following two model sentences are already printed on the Student Page:

> The circuit rider was from Boston.
> The circuit rider rode all over the state of Wisconsin.

Ask the student to look carefully at the sentences. Remind her that the names of states and cities are capitalized. Ask her to point to the capital letters that begin the names "Boston" and "Wisconsin."

Choose whichever sentence is appropriate to the student's handwriting ability. Watch the student as she writes in pencil. If she begins to make an error, gently stop her and ask her to look at the model again.

Day Four: Narration Exercise and Copywork   *Student Page 32*

Pull out Student Page 32. Write the student's name and the date for her as she watches, or ask her to write the name and date independently.

Tell the student that the following passage from *Caddie Woodlawn* happens after the circuit rider leaves. Now the children are looking forward to their uncle's visit, which happens every year.

The next day the circuit rider rode away on his horse....and life went on again as usual. But now the children began to talk about when Uncle Edmund would come, for Uncle Edmund always came with the pigeons in the fall. He made his annual visit when the shooting was at its best, for he was an eager if not a very skillful sportsman.

Mrs. Woodlawn sighed. "No one can say that I am not a devoted sister," she said, "but the prospect of a visit from Edmund always fills me with alarm. My house is turned upside down, my children behave like wild things, there is nothing but noise and confusion."

"But Ma—" cried Tom.

"Don't Ma me, my child," said Mrs. Woodlawn calmly.

"But, Mother," persisted Tom, defending his hero. "Uncle Edmund knows the most tricks—"

"And jokes!" cried Caddie.

"Remember when he put the hairbrush in Caddie's bed?" shouted Warren.

"And the time he put a frog in a covered dish on the supper table, and when Mrs. Conroy lifted the cover—"

"That is enough, Tom," said his mother. "We remember Uncle Edmund's tricks very well, and I've no doubt we'll soon see more of them."

But she looked forward to her younger brother's coming just the same, and when the pigeons came and there was no Uncle Edmund everyone felt surprised and concerned.

One night when they went to bed the sky was clear and the woods were still. But when they awoke in the crisp autumn morning the air was full of the noise of wings, and flocks of birds flew like clouds across the sun. The passenger pigeons were on their way south. They filled the trees in the woods. They came down in the fields and gardens, feeding on whatever seeds and grains they could find. The last birds kept flying over those which were feeding in front, in order to come at new ground, so that the flock seemed to roll along like a great moving cloud.

"The pigeons have come!" shouted the little Woodlawns. "The pigeons have come!" Even baby Joe waved his arms and shouted.

—From *Caddie Woodlawn*
by Carol Ryrie Brink

Ask the following questions. Remind the student to answer you in complete sentences. If she answers in a fragment, turn the fragment into a complete sentence, say it to her, and then ask her to repeat this sentence back to you. If she cannot answer a question, read her the part of the passage that contains the answer, and then ask the question again.

Instructor: Uncle Edmund comes in the fall. What kind of birds come at the same time?
Student: *Pigeons come at the same time.*

Instructor: Who is Uncle Edmund's sister?
Student: *Mrs. Woodlawn is his sister.*

Instructor: What did Uncle Edmund put in Caddie's bed?
Student: *He put a hairbrush in her bed.*

Instructor: What did he put in a covered dish on the supper table?
Student: *He put a frog in the dish.*

Instructor: Did Uncle Edmund come when the pigeons came?
Student: *No, he did not.*

Instructor: What was the baby in the Woodlawn family named?
Student: *He was named Joe.*

Ask, "What is one thing you remember about the passage?" Write the student's answer down on the "Instructor" lines of Student Page 32 as she watches. This answer can be the same as one of the answers above.

Now ask the student to copy the sentence in pencil on the "Student" lines below the model. If the sentence is too long for comfort, she can copy only the first six to eight words.

WEEK 9

DAY ONE: Copywork   *Student Page 33*

Focus: *Capitalizing first (proper) names and names of states*

Pull out Student Page 33. Write the student's name and the date for him as he watches, or ask him to write the name and date independently.

The following two model sentences are already printed on the Student Page:

> The school bus honked from the road.
> The teacher asked Fern to name the capital of Pennsylvania.

Ask the student to look carefully at the sentences. Explain that this week's readings come from the book *Charlotte's Web*, by E. B. White. *Charlotte's Web* tells the story of a little girl named Fern and her pet pig Wilbur. Fern and Wilbur live in the state of Pennsylvania.

Tell the student that the names of states are **proper nouns.** Ask the student to point to the name of the state of Pennsylvania, and the capital letter that begins the name of the state. Also ask the student to point to the name "Fern," which is the first (proper) name of Wilbur's owner.

Choose whichever sentence is appropriate to the student's handwriting ability. Watch the student as he writes in pencil. If he begins to make an error, gently stop him and ask him to look at the model again.

DAY TWO: Narration Exercise   *Student Page 34*

Pull out Student Page 34. Write the student's name and the date for him as he watches, or ask him to write the name and date independently.

Explain to the student that Mr. Arable and his wife live on a farm, where a litter of pigs has just been born. Mr. Arable wants to get rid of the smallest pig, the runt of the litter. But his daughter Fern begs him to spare the pig's life. Mr. Arable agrees, and Fern and her older brother Avery then head off to school.

> The school bus honked from the road.
>
> "Run!" commanded Mrs. Arable, taking the pig from Fern and slipping a doughnut into her hand. Avery grabbed his gun and another doughnut.
>
> The children ran out to the road and climbed into the bus. Fern took no notice of the others in the bus. She just sat and stared out of the window, thinking what a blissful world it was and how lucky she was to have entire charge of a pig. By the time the bus reached the school, Fern had named her pet, selecting the most beautiful name she could think of.
>
> "Its name is Wilbur," she whispered to herself.
>
> She was still thinking about the pig when the teacher said: "Fern, what is the capital of Pennsylvania?"
>
> "Wilbur," Fern replied, dreamily. The pupils giggled. Fern blushed.

—From *Charlotte's Web*
by E. B. White

Ask the following questions. Remind the student to answer you in complete sentences. If he answers in a fragment, turn the fragment into a complete sentence, say it to him, and then ask him to repeat this sentence back to you. If he cannot answer a question, read him the part of the passage that contains the answer, and then ask the question again.

Instructor: What noise does the school bus make?
Student: *The school bus honks.*

Instructor: What does Mrs. Arable command Fern and Avery to do?
Student: *She tells them to run so that they won't miss the bus.*

Instructor: What do Fern and Avery eat for breakfast?
Student: *They each have a doughnut.*

Instructor: What did Fern do on her bus ride to school?
Student: *She looked out the window and thought about how lucky she was to be able to take care of the pig.*

Instructor: What did Fern name the pig?
Student: *She named him Wilbur.*

Instructor: When the teacher asked Fern what the capital of Pennsylvania is, what did she say?
Student: *She said, "Wilbur."*

Instructor: What did the other students do when Fern said this?
Student: *They giggled.*

Ask, "What is one thing you remember about the passage?" Write the student's answer down on Student Page 34 as he watches. This answer can be the same as one of the answers above.

DAY THREE: Copywork   *Student Page 35*

Focus: *Review capitalizing first (proper) names*

Pull out Student Page 35. Write the student's name and the date for him as he watches, or ask him to write the name and date independently.
The following two model sentences are already printed on the Student Page:

> She named him Wilbur.
> Fern took no notice of the others on the bus.

Ask the student to look carefully at the sentences and to point out the first (proper) names in each sentence.
Choose whichever sentence is appropriate to the student's handwriting ability. Watch the student as he writes in pencil. If he begins to make an error, gently stop him and ask him to look at the model again.

DAY FOUR: Narration Exercise and Copywork   *Student Page 36*

Pull out Student Page 36. Write the student's name and the date for him as he watches, or ask him to write the name and date independently.
Read the following passage out loud to the student.

> Fern loved Wilbur more than anything. She loved to stroke him, to feed him, to put him to bed. Every morning, as soon as she got up, she warmed his milk, tied his bib on, and held the bottle for him. Every afternoon, when the schoolbus stopped in front of her house, she jumped out and ran to the kitchen to fix another bottle for him. She fed him again at suppertime, and again just before going to bed. Mrs. Arable gave him a feeding around noontime each day, when Fern was away in school. Wilbur loved his milk, and he was never happier than when Fern was warming up a bottle for him. He would stand and gaze up at her with adoring eyes.

> For the first few days of his life, Wilbur was allowed to live in a box near the stove in the kitchen. Then, when Mrs. Arable complained, he was moved to a bigger box in the woodshed. At two weeks of age, he was moved outdoors. It was apple-blossom time, and the days were getting warmer. Mr. Arable fixed a small yard specially for Wilbur under an apple tree, and gave him a large wooden box full of straw, with a doorway cut in it so he could walk in and out as he pleased.

—From *Charlotte's Web*
by E. B. White

Ask the following questions. Remind the student to answer you in complete sentences. If he answers in a fragment, turn the fragment into a complete sentence, say it to him, and then ask him to repeat this sentence back to you. If he cannot answer a question, read him the part of the passage that contains the answer, and then ask the question again.

Instructor: Fern loved to care for Wilbur. Can you remember one of the things she did for him before she left for school?
Student: *She warmed his milk, tied his bib on, and held his bottle for him.*

Instructor: What did she do as soon as the schoolbus stopped in front of her house?
Student: *She ran to fix him another bottle.*

Instructor: How many more times did she feed him during the day?
Student: *She fed him two more times (at suppertime and before bed).*

Instructor: When did Mrs. Arable feed him?
Student: *She fed him at noontime.*

Instructor: Can you add all those times together and tell me how often Wilbur was fed?
Student: *He was fed five times.* [You may need to prompt the student for this answer.]

Instructor: What did Wilbur do when Fern warmed up a bottle for him?
Student: *He gazed up at her with adoring eyes.*

Instructor: Where did Wilbur live at first?
Student: *Wilbur lived in a box near the stove in the kitchen.*

Instructor: Where did he have to move after a few days of living in the kitchen?
Student: *He had to move to a bigger box out in the woodshed.*

Ask, "What is one thing you remember about the passage?" Write the student's answer down on the "Instructor" lines of Student Page 36 as he watches. This answer can be the same as one of the answers above.

Now ask the student to copy the sentence in pencil on the "Student" lines below the model. If the sentence is too long for comfort, he can copy only the first six to eight words.

WEEK 10

DAY ONE: Copywork   *Student Page 37*

Focus: *Capitalizing names of states; capitalizing first and last names*

Pull out Student Page 37. Write the student's name and the date for her as she watches, or ask her to write the name and date independently.

The following two model sentences are already printed on the Student Page:

> Davy Crockett was born in Tennessee.
> Davy Crockett lived in Tennessee, but he wanted to explore the
>   state of Texas.

Ask the student to look carefully at the sentences. Explain that these sentences are about Davy Crockett, an explorer and soldier who lived in the early 1800s. Davy Crockett grew up in Tennessee, but when he was fifty years old, he went down to Texas because he wanted to see what this new United States territory was like.

Remind the student that the names of states are **proper nouns**. "State" is a common noun—it could refer to any of the fifty states in the United States. But each particular state has its own special name. Those names are proper nouns. Have the student point to the name of the states, and the capital letter that begins the name of each state. Ask the student to point to the other proper nouns in the sentences (the name "Davy Crockett").

Choose whichever sentence is appropriate to the student's handwriting ability. Watch the student as she writes in pencil. If she begins to make an error, gently stop her and ask her to look at the model again.

DAY TWO: Narration Exercise   *Student Page 38*

Pull out Student Page 38. Write the student's name and the date for her as she watches, or ask her to write the name and date independently.

Read the following passage about Davy Crockett's childhood out loud to the student. (The ellipses represent sentences that have been left out in order to simplify and condense the selection.)

> Mrs. Crockett was firm. "Every boy and man on this Tennessee clearing gets a haircut this day. You are all as shaggy as Indian colts after a hard winter."
>
> Seven-year-old Davy looked at his four older brothers. Long hair hung around the ears and down the neck of each one. It had felt warm and comfortable all winter. Not even Pa had had a haircut since fall.....

Ma had chosen a big stump near the house for her barber chair. First Pa was seated there to have his hair cut. Then Jason, Jim, and Bill each took his turn.

Ma placed the pewter bowl she had brought all the way from Maryland over each head in turn. Her shears had come from Maryland, too, and Ma was very proud of them. The blades were heavy and long. Pa or Jason honed them sharp for her, but Ma always stood by to see that they did the job right....

Davy begged, "Please, Ma, cut my hair tomorrow. Look, Ma, let me go swimming now and tomorrow I'll sit just as still as Bill did."

Ma would not listen—just put the bowl on Davy's head....

The shears looked bigger and brighter and sharper close up. They made a great clacking noise. When the cold metal touched his ear Davy gave a yell and jumped. He would have run away, but Ma had a firm grip on his head.

"Sit still, Davy. I haven't cut off an ear yet."

The big shears clicked above Davy's ears and across the back of his head. Their flat blades felt cold against his scalp as Ma clipped the long hair away.

—From *Davy Crockett, Young Rifleman*
by Aileen Wells Parks

Ask the following questions. Remind the student to answer you in complete sentences. If she answers in a fragment, turn the fragment into a complete sentence, say it to her, and then ask her to repeat this sentence back to you. If she cannot answer a question, read her the part of the passage that contains the answer, and then ask the question again.

Instructor: What state did the Crockett family live in?
Student: *They lived in Tennessee.*

Instructor: What state did Davy Crockett's mother come from?
Student: *She came from Maryland.*

Instructor: Why did Davy's hair need cutting so badly?
Student: *It had been growing all winter.*

Instructor: What did Davy's mother use for her barber chair?
Student: *She used a stump.*

Instructor: What did she put on Davy's head?
Student: *She put a bowl on his head.*

Instructor: What did Davy's mother tell him to reassure him when he jumped and yelled?
Student: *She said, "I haven't cut off an ear yet."*

Ask, "What is one thing you remember about the passage?" Write the student's answer down on Student Page 38 as she watches. This answer can be the same as one of the answers above.

DAY THREE: Copywork

Focus: Capitalizing other proper names

Pull out Student Page 39. Write the student's name and the date for her as she watches, or ask her to write the name and date independently.

The following two model sentences are already printed on it:

> Sacagawea belonged to the Shoshoni tribe.
> Sacagawea helped Meriwether Lewis and William Clark explore the Missouri River.

Ask the student to look carefully at the sentences. Explain that these sentences are about Sacagawea (pronounced sah-kah-gah-wee-ah, with a hard *g* sound), a young Native American woman who was born into the Shoshoni tribe. When she was 17, Sacagawea helped to guide two explorers named Meriwether Lewis and William Clark up the Missouri River and across the Rocky Mountains.

Tell the student that "Shoshoni" is a **proper noun** because it is the name of a particular tribe. "Missouri River" is a **proper noun** because it is the name of a particular river. Ask the student to point to the capital letters that begin each proper noun in the sentence.

Choose whichever sentence is appropriate to the student's handwriting ability. Watch the student as she writes in pencil. If she begins to make an error, gently stop her and ask her to look at the model again.

DAY FOUR: Narration Exercise and Copywork

Pull out Student Page 40. Write the student's name and the date for her as she watches, or ask her to write the name and date independently.

Read the following passage about Sacagawea's childhood out loud to the student.

> Sacagawea came out of the tepee into the bright sunlight. Her black hair hung about her bare shoulders. Her eyes were brown and so was her skin. An Indian girl of the Shoshoni tribe, she was about seven years old.
> Her mother was sitting on the ground in front of the tepee.
> "What are you doing, Mother?" the girl asked.
> "Use your eyes, Bird Girl," said her mother. "Let them answer your questions." She shook out the deerskin on which she was working. It was almost shapeless, but Bird Girl could see that it looked like a soft slipper.
> "Oh, I see!" Bird Girl said. "Big Brother's moccasins!"
> "I am mending them," her mother explained.
> "Where is he going?"
> Travels Fast—he was several years older than Sacagawea—had come up and was listening.

"Hunting," he said proudly.

Sacagawea opened her brown eyes wide. Hunting! That meant he was almost grown-up. She felt a bit envious.

"Where are you going? When will you start? May I go, too?"

Travels Fast laughed. "How can I answer three questions at once?" he asked teasingly. "No, hunting trips are not for girls," he went on. "You will be fast asleep when I start off in that direction."

He waved his hand toward one of the rocky hills. These hills were all around the valley where the tepees or skin tents of the tribe were. The valley was high up in the Rocky Mountains, in what is now the state of Wyoming. But this was in 1794, long before Wyoming became a state. At that time the Shoshoni had never even heard of the United States, which was a very new country. Indeed, no one of the whole tribe had ever seen a white man.

—From *Sacagawea: American Pathfinder*
by Flora Warren Seymour

Ask the following questions. Remind the student to answer you in complete sentences. If she answers in a fragment, turn the fragment into a complete sentence, say it to her, and then ask her to repeat this sentence back to you. If she cannot answer a question, read her the part of the passage that contains the answer, and then ask the question again.

Instructor: What tribe did Sacagawea belong to?
Student: *She belonged to the Shoshoni tribe.*

Instructor: What name did Sacagawea's mother call her?
Student: *Her mother called her Bird Girl.*

Instructor: What was Sacagawea's mother mending?
Student: *She was mending moccasins.*

Instructor: What was Sacagawea's brother named?
Student: *He was named Travels Fast.*

Instructor: What sort of trip was he going on?
Student: *He was going on a hunting trip.*

Instructor: Sacagawea's family lived in the Rocky Mountains, on land that eventually became part of an American state. Do you remember the name of the state?
Student: *The state is Wyoming.*

Ask, "What is one thing you remember about the passage?" Write the student's answer down on the "Instructor" lines of Student Page 40 as she watches. This answer can be the same as one of the answers above.

Now ask the student to copy the sentence in pencil on the "Student" lines below the model. If the sentence is too long for comfort, she can copy only the first six to eight words.

WEEK 11

DAY ONE: Copywork   *Student Page 41*

Focus: *Capitalizing names of states, and first and last names*

Pull out Student Page 41. Write the student's name and the date for him as he watches, or ask him to write the name and date independently.

The following two model sentences are already printed on it:

> Louis is a musician.
> He came here from Montana with Sam Beaver.

Ask the student to look carefully at the sentences. While he is examining the sentences, explain that these sentences are from *The Trumpet of the Swan,* by E. B. White. The book is about a young trumpeter swan named Louis who is born without a voice. A young boy named Sam Beaver becomes his friend. Since he can't speak, Louis learns how to write on a slate—and also how to play a real trumpet.

Ask the student to point to the **proper nouns** in the sentences. If necessary, remind him that "Montana" is the proper name of a state.

Choose whichever sentence is appropriate to the student's handwriting ability. Watch the student as he writes in pencil. If he begins to make an error, gently stop him and ask him to look at the model again.

DAY TWO: Narration Exercise   *Student Page 42*

Pull out Student Page 42. Write the student's name and the date for him as he watches, or ask him to write the name and date independently.

Tell the student that the following scene takes place near the beginning of the book. Louis and his brothers and sisters have just hatched out of their eggs, and their parents are taking them for their very first swim. Sam Beaver is sitting quietly by the pond, watching them. Explain that a "cob" is a male swan, and that "cygnet" is the name for a baby swan.

> Like all fathers, the cob wanted to show off his children to somebody. So he led the cygnets to where Sam was. They all stepped out of the water and stood in front of the boy—all but the mother swan. She stayed behind.
>
> "Ko-hoh!" said the cob.
>
> "Hello!" said Sam, who hadn't expected anything like this and hardly dared breathe.
>
> The first cygnet looked at Sam and said, "Beep." The second cygnet looked at Sam and said, "Beep." The third cygnet greeted Sam the same way. So did the fourth. The fifth cygnet was different. He opened his mouth but

> didn't say a thing. He made an effort to say beep, but no sound came. So instead, he stuck his little neck out, took hold of one of Sam's shoelaces, and gave it a pull. He tugged the lace for a moment. It came untied. Then he let it go. It was like a greeting. Sam grinned.
>
> The cob now looked worried. He ran his long white neck between the cygnets and the boy and guided the babies back to the water and to their mother.
>
> "Follow me!" said the cob. And he led them off, full of grace and bursting with pride.

—From *The Trumpet of the Swan*
by E. B. White

Ask the following questions. Remind the student to answer you in complete sentences. If he answers in a fragment, turn the fragment into a complete sentence, say it to him, and then ask him to repeat this sentence back to you. If he cannot answer a question, read him the part of the passage that contains the answer, and then ask the question again.

Instructor: Which parent took the cygnets to see Sam Beaver—their mother or their father?
Student: *Their father took them.*

Instructor: What is a male swan called?
Student: *A male swan is called a cob.*

Instructor: What did most of the cygnets say to Sam?
Student: *They said "Beep."*

Instructor: Why was the fifth cygnet different?
Student: *He couldn't say anything.*

Instructor: What did he do instead?
Student: *He pulled on Sam's shoelace.*

Instructor: Where did the cob take the babies after they met Sam?
Student: *He took them back to the water OR back to their mother.*

Ask, "What is one thing you remember about the passage?" Write the student's answer down on Student Page 42 as he watches. This answer can be the same as one of the answers above.

Day Three: Copywork   *Student Page 43*

Focus: *Capitalizing names of states and cities*

Pull out Student Page 43. Write the student's name and the date for him as he watches, or ask him to write the name and date independently.

The following two model sentences are already printed on it:

Louis had no trouble finding Philadelphia.
They flew south across Maryland and Virginia.

Ask the student to look carefully at the sentences. While he is examining the sentences, explain that, in the story, Louis decides to leave his home and explore other places.

Ask the student to point to the **proper nouns** in the sentences. Tell the student that these nouns name two states and one city. If necessary, tell him which names are states and which one is a city. Ask him to point to the capital letters that begin each name.

Choose whichever sentence is appropriate to the student's handwriting ability. Watch the student as he writes in pencil. If he begins to make an error, gently stop him and ask him to look at the model again.

DAY FOUR: Narration Exercise and Copywork   *Student Page 44*

Pull out Student Page 44. Write the student's name and the date for him as he watches, or ask him to write the name and date independently.

Read the following passage out loud to the student. In this scene, Louis's father has realized that his young son can't speak. He decides to go and find Louis a trumpet in the nearby city of Billings, Montana.

> Toward the end of the afternoon, the cob looked ahead and in the distance saw the churches and factories and shops and homes of Billings. He decided to act quickly and boldly. He circled the city once, looking for a music store. Suddenly he spied one. It had a very big, wide window, solid glass. The cob flew lower and circled so that he could get a better look. He gazed into the store. He saw a drum painted gold. He saw a fancy guitar with an electric cord. He saw a small piano. He saw banjos, horns, violins, mandolins, cymbals, saxophones, marimbaphones, cellos, and many other instruments. Then he saw what he wanted: he saw a brass trumpet hanging by a a red cord.
>
> "Now is my time to act!" he said to himself. "Now is my moment for risking everything on one bold move, however shocking it may be to my sensibilities, however offensive it may be to the laws that govern the lives of men. Here I go! May good luck go with me!"
>
> With that, the old cob set his wings for a dive. He aimed straight at the big window. He held his neck stiff and straight, waiting for the crash. He dove swiftly and hit the window going full speed. The glass broke. The noise was terrific. The whole store shook. Musical instruments fell to the floor. Glass flew everywhere. A salesgirl fainted. The cob felt a twinge of pain as a jagged piece of broken glass cut into his shoulder, but he grabbed the trumpet in his beak, turned sharply in the air, flew back through the

> hole in the window, and began climbing fast over the roofs of Billings. A few drops of blood fell to the ground below. His shoulder hurt. But he had succeeded in getting what he had come for. Held firmly in his bill, its red cord dangling, was a beautiful brass trumpet.

—From *The Trumpet of the Swan*
by E. B. White

Ask the following questions. Remind the student to answer you in complete sentences. If he answers in a fragment, turn the fragment into a complete sentence, say it to him, and then ask him to repeat this sentence back to you. If he cannot answer a question, read him the part of the passage that contains the answer, and then ask the question again.

Instructor: What was the cob looking for, as he circled the city?
Student: *He was looking for a music store.*

Instructor: Can you name three things that the cob saw inside the store?
Student: *He saw a drum, a guitar, a piano, banjos, horns, violins, mandolins, cymbals, saxophones, marimbaphones, and cellos.*

Instructor: How did the cob get into the store?
Student: *He broke through the window.*

Instructor: Did he hurt himself? Where?
Student: *Yes, he hurt his shoulder.*

Instructor: When he flew away, what was he holding in his bill?
Student: *He was holding a beautiful brass trumpet.*

Ask, "What is one thing you remember about the passage?" Write the student's answer down on the "Instructor" lines of Student Page 44 as he watches. This answer can be the same as one of the answers above.

Now ask the student to copy the sentence in pencil on the "Student" lines below the model. If the sentence is too long for comfort, he can copy only the first eight to ten words.

WEEK 12

DAY ONE: Copywork   *Student Page 45*

Focus: *Capitalizing days of the week; beginning capitals and ending periods*

Pull out Student Page 45. Write the student's name and the date for her as she watches, or ask her to write the name and date independently.

The following two model sentences are already printed on it:

Today is Monday, today is Monday.
Today is Wednesday, today is Wednesday. Wednesday is soup day.

Ask the student to look carefully at the sentences. While she is examining them, tell the student that these sentences are from an old, old song called "Today Is Monday." The song explains what the family does on every day of the week.

Remind the student that there are seven days in a week—Sunday, Monday, Tuesday, Wednesday, Thursday, Friday, and Saturday. The names of the days of the week are **proper nouns.** Have the student point to the name of each day and the capital letter that begins each name.

Choose whichever sentence is appropriate to the student's handwriting ability. Watch the student as she writes in pencil. If she begins to make an error, gently stop her and ask her to look at the model again.

DAY TWO: Narration Exercise   *Student Page 46*

Pull out Student Page 46. Write the student's name and the date for her as she watches, or ask her to write the name and date independently.

Explain to the student that you are going to read her the verses of an old song. She needs to listen very carefully, because you will ask her to try to remember what the song says about each day.

Today is Monday, today is Monday.
Monday, wash day.
All you happy people, we sing the same to you!

Today is Tuesday, today is Tuesday.
Tuesday, iron.
Monday, wash day.
All you happy people, we sing the same to you!

Today is Wednesday, today is Wednesday.
Wednesday, soup.
Tuesday, iron.
Monday, wash day.
All you happy people, we sing the same to you!

Today is Thursday, today is Thursday.
Thursday, roast beef.
Wednesday, soup.
Tuesday, iron.
Monday, wash day.
All you happy people, we sing the same to you!

Today is Friday, today is Friday.
Friday, clean.
Thursday, roast beef.
Wednesday, soup.
Tuesday, iron.
Monday, wash day.
All you happy people, we sing the same to you!

Today is Saturday, today is Saturday.
Saturday, bake.
Friday, clean.
Thursday, roast beef.
Wednesday, soup.
Tuesday, iron.
Monday, wash day.
All you happy people, we sing the same to you!

Today is Sunday, today is Sunday.
Sunday, church.
Saturday, bake.
Friday, clean.
Thursday, roast beef.
Wednesday, soup.
Tuesday, iron.
Monday, wash day.
All you happy people, we sing the same to you!

—"Today Is Monday"

Ask the following questions. Remind the student to answer you in complete sentences. If she answers in a fragment, turn the fragment into a complete sentence, say it to her, and then ask her to repeat this sentence back to you. If she cannot answer a question, read her the part of the song that contains the answer, and then ask the question again.

Instructor: What happens on Monday?
Student: *Monday is wash day.*

Instructor: What happens to the laundry on Tuesday?
Student: *The laundry is ironed.*

Instructor: What does the family eat on Wednesday?
Student: *The family eats soup.*

Instructor: The family eats soup on Wednesday because, many years ago, it took the mother all day on Tuesday to do the ironing—so she didn't have time to cook anything else! What does the family eat on Thursday?
Student: *The family eats roast beef on Thursday.*

Instructor: What does the family do on Friday?
Student: *On Friday the family cleans.*

Instructor: What happens on Saturday?
Student: *Saturday is bake day.*

Instructor: What does the family do on Sunday?
Student: *On Sunday the family goes to church.*

Ask, "What is one thing you remember about the passage?" Write the student's answer down on Student Page 46 as she watches. This answer can be the same as one of the answers above.

DAY THREE: Copywork

Student Page 47

Focus: *Capitalizing days of the week*

Pull out Student Page 47. Write the student's name and the date for her as she watches, or ask her to write the name and date independently.

The following two model sentences are already printed on it:

On Thursday we eat roast beef.
Today is Friday. On Friday we clean the house from top to bottom.

Ask the student to look carefully at the sentences. Remind her that the names of the days of the week are **proper nouns** and should be capitalized.

Choose whichever sentence is appropriate to the student's handwriting ability. Watch the student as she writes in pencil. If she begins to make an error, gently stop her and ask her to look at the model again.

DAY FOUR: Narration Exercise and Copywork

Student Page 48

Pull out Student Page 48. Write the student's name and the date for her as she watches, or ask her to write the name and date independently.

Tell the student that today's narration is another very old poem. It is a "nursery rhyme"— an old poem which has been told to children for so long that we no longer know who wrote it. When we don't know who wrote a poem or story, we say that it was written by "Anonymous." "Anonymous" means no name is known.

The student will need to pay close attention to this rhyme so that she can answer the questions afterwards!

Old Mother Hubbard, she went to the cupboard,
To get her poor dog a bone.
When she got there, the cupboard was bare,

And so the poor dog had none.
She went to the baker's to buy him some bread,
But when she came back the poor dog was dead.
She went to the undertaker's to buy him a coffin,
And when she came back the dog was laughing.
She went to the draper's to buy him some linen,
And when she came back the good dog was spinning.
She went to the hosier's to buy him some hose,
And when she came back he was dressed in his clothes.
The dame made a curtsy, the dog made a bow,
The dame said, "Your servant." The dog said "Bow-wow."
She went to the hatter's to buy him a hat,
And when she came back he was feeding the cat.
She went to the tailor's to buy him a coat,
And when she came back he was riding the goat.
She went to the barber's to buy him a wig,
And when she came back he was dancing a jig.
She went to the butcher's to get him some tripe,
And when she came back he was smoking a pipe.
She went to the fish-shop to buy him some fish,
And when she came back he was washing the dish.
She went to the tavern for white wine and red,
And when she came back the dog stood on his head.

—"Old Mother Hubbard"
by Anonymous

Ask the following questions. Remind the student to answer you in complete sentences. If she answers in a fragment, turn the fragment into a complete sentence, say it to her, and then ask her to repeat this sentence back to you. If she cannot answer a question, read her the part of the rhyme that contains the answer, and then ask the question again.

Instructor: What did Mother Hubbard want to get out of the cupboard for her dog?
Student: She wanted to get the dog a bone.

Instructor: What did she buy at the baker's?
Student: She bought bread.

Instructor: When she came back from buying him a coffin, was the dog dead?
Student: No, he was laughing.

Instructor: See if you can complete this rhyme. "She went to the hosier's to buy him some hose, and when she came back he was dressed in…"
Student: His clothes. [The student may answer this question with a phrase rather than a complete sentence.]

Instructor: When Mother Hubbard said, "Your servant," what did the dog say?
Student: The dog said, "Bow-wow."

Instructor: Mother Hubbard bought the dog a hat. When she came back, what was he feeding?
Student: *He was feeding the cat.*

Instructor: What animal did the dog go for a ride on?
Student: *He rode on a goat.*

Instructor: After Mother Hubbard bought the dog a wig, what kind of dance did he do?
Student: *He danced a jig.*

Instructor: See if you can complete this rhyme. "She went to the fish-shop to buy him some fish, and when she came back…"
Student: *He was washing the dish.*

Instructor: What was the very last thing the dog did in the poem?
Student: *He stood on his head.*

Ask, "What is one thing you remember about the passage?" Write the student's answer down on the "Instructor" lines of Student Page 48 as she watches. This answer can be the same as one of the answers above.

Now ask the student to copy the sentence in pencil on the "Student" lines below the model. If the sentence is too long for comfort, she can copy only the first eight to ten words.

WEEK 13

DAY ONE: Copywork   *Student Page 49*

Focus: *Capitalizing days of the week*

Pull out Student Page 49. Write the student's name and the date for him as he watches, or ask him to write the name and date independently.

The following two model sentences are already printed on the Student Page:

> Rain is for Saturday and Sunday.
> Good weather is for Monday, Tuesday, Wednesday, Thursday, and Friday.

Ask the student to look carefully at the sentences. Tell him that these sentences are from *The Saturdays,* by Elizabeth Enright. In this book, four children decide to form a club called the Independent Saturday Afternoon Adventure Club. They agree that they will combine all of their allowances together, and each Saturday, one of them will take the entire amount and have an adventure. The oldest boy, Rush, complains that it always rains on the weekends (Saturday and Sunday) and holidays—and that school days (when the children have to be inside) are always beautiful.

Remind the student that there are seven days in a week—Sunday, Monday, Tuesday, Wednesday, Thursday, Friday, and Saturday. The name of each day is a **proper noun,** so each name begins with a capital letter.

Choose whichever sentence is appropriate to the student's handwriting ability. Watch the student as he writes in pencil. If he begins to make an error, gently stop him and ask him to look at the model again.

DAY TWO: Narration Exercise   *Student Page 50*

Pull out Student Page 50. Write the student's name and the date for him as he watches, or ask him to write the name and date independently.

Tell the student that the following selection is from *The Saturdays,* by Elizabeth Enright. The four children who form the Independent Saturday Afternoon Adventure Club all belong to the same family—the Melendy family. They live with their father and their housekeeper in New York City, about seventy years ago. The oldest, Mona, is thirteen; Rush is twelve; Miranda (nicknamed Randy) is ten; and Oliver is six. They call their housekeeper "Cuffy," and their nickname for their playroom is "the Office."

> All the Melendy children had their own jobs. They each had not one but several. For instance, they made their own beds and took weekly turns at cleaning the Office (all except Oliver, of course). And the cleaning had to be thorough. Under Cuffy's eagle eye there could be no nonsense such as sweeping things under things, or shaking the mop out the window, or dusting only where it showed. It had to be well done. In addition to these were the special jobs. Rush shined all the shoes, took care of the fuse box, repaired the radio when necessary, and was a sort of plumber's assistant.... Mona helped Cuffy with the mending and ironing, and had the entire responsibility of keeping the living room tidy. Randy always set the dinner table and dried the dishes, as well as sorting the laundry and making out the lists. Even Oliver had his chores. He had to water all the plants, and feed the fish and his turtle, and see that the clay in the tub was kept moist.
>
> So between jobs and school and amusing themselves, life for the Melendys rarely contained a dull moment.
>
> This, however, was one of them.
>
> "I'm so b-o-o-o-o-red!" groaned Randy, lifting one foot in the air and letting it drop heavily as though simply unable to sustain the weight of her boredom.
>
> "You and me, both," agreed Rush.
>
> "And I'm bored listening to you complain," complained Mona, slapping her book together.

—From *The Saturdays*
by Elizabeth Enright

Ask the following questions. Remind the student to answer you in complete sentences. If he answers in a fragment, turn the fragment into a complete sentence, say it to him, and then ask him to repeat this sentence back to you. If he cannot answer a question, read him the part of the passage that contains the answer, and then ask the question again.

Instructor: What did each child do to his or her own bed?
Student: *Each child made his own bed.*

Instructor: All of the children except the youngest took turns doing one particular job. Can you remember what that job was?
Student: *They took turns cleaning the Office (the playroom).*

Instructor: The housekeeper, Cuffy, made sure that the children did a good job. There were three things that she did not allow them to do when they cleaned. Can you remember one of those things?
Student: *She did not allow them to sweep things under things, shake the mop out of the window, or dust only where it showed.*

Instructor: Can you remember two of the four jobs that Rush, the older boy, did?
Student: *He shined the shoes, took care of the fuse box, fixed the radio, and did plumbing.*

Instructor: Can you remember two of the three jobs that Mona, the older girl, had?
Student: *She helped with mending, helped with ironing, and kept the living room tidy.*

Instructor: Can you remember two of the four jobs that the younger girl, Randy (Miranda), did?
Student: *She set the table, dried the dishes, sorted laundry, and made lists.*

Instructor: What are two of the jobs that the littlest child, Oliver, had?
Student: *He watered the plants, fed the fish, fed his turtle, and kept the clay damp.*

Instructor: What problem did all the children have?
Student: *They were bored.*

Ask, "What is one thing you remember about the passage?" Write the student's answer down on Student Page 50 as he watches. This answer can be the same as one of the answers above.

DAY THREE: Copywork   *Student Page 51*

Focus: *Capitalizing days of the week and holidays*

Pull out Student Page 51. Write the student's name and the date for him as he watches, or ask him to write the name and date independently.

The following two model sentences are already printed on the Student Page:

> Saturday dawned much the same as any other day.
> When Randy woke up, she had the same feeling in her stomach that she always had on Christmas Day.

Ask the student to look carefully at the sentences. The first sentence has the name "Saturday" in it. This name is capitalized because it is the name of a day of the week. The second sentence also has the name of a day in it—Christmas Day. "Christmas Day" is the name of a holiday. It is a **proper noun.** We capitalize the names of holidays because they name *particular* days of the year.

Choose whichever sentence is appropriate to the student's handwriting ability. Watch the student as he writes in pencil. If he begins to make an error, gently stop him and ask him to look at the model again.

If necessary, the student may practice forming commas at the bottom of Student Page 51.

DAY FOUR: Narration Exercise and Copywork   *Student Page 52*

Pull out Student Page 52. Write the student's name and the date for him as he watches, or ask him to write the name and date independently.

Read the following passage out loud to the student. Tell him that Oliver, who is six years old, decides that he is going to have a Saturday adventure too—so he sets out all by himself with his whole allowance to go to the circus.

It was easy when he got there. He just stood in a long line of grownups and children and held tight to his dimes and listened to what the people in front him said when they got to the window. So when he got there he was able to say "One, please. The kind that costs one dollar," and count out ten dimes slowly and carefully. The man behind the window had to peer down in order to see him at all. Then holding his ticket tightly he followed close behind a large family and tried hard to look like one of them.

"Like to hold your own ticket, eh, sonny?" said the ticket man.

"Yes, I do," replied Oliver, and entered....It was wonderful. It smelled of elephants the minute you got in, even before you came to the real circus part. Breathing the smell deeply, Oliver climbed some steps that a uniformed man told him to, and then walked along a corridor that another uniformed man told him to. He thought he heard a lion roar some place, and his feet crunched on peanut shells. It was very exciting. Finally he came to the right door, entered it, and found himself in another world. It was a vast world, carpeted with blue sawdust and walled with thousands of faces. A complicated web of cables and rope ladders and nets rose from the huge arena to misty reigions high overhead. On the blue sawdust at the bottom there were three large caged rings, and in each of these rings the most extraordinary things were happening.

"This way, Bud," said the usher, steering the bedazzled Oliver to a seat. Oliver sat down without knowing that he did so. After a long time he removed his coat and cap blindly, never taking his eyes off the ring nearest him. In it three lions, two bears, and a black leopard were climbing ladders, while on high gold stools seven other lions sat and snarled and batted with their paws at their trainer who was the bravest man in the world and wore a red coat. He could make those animals do anything. Before he was through, one of the bears was pushing the other in a huge baby carriage while all the lions, on a bridge overhead, sat up on their hind legs and begged.

—From *The Saturdays*
by Elizabeth Enright

Ask the following questions. Remind the student to answer you in complete sentences. If he answers in a fragment, turn the fragment into a complete sentence, say it to him, and then ask him to repeat this sentence back to you. If he cannot answer a question, read him the part of the passage that contains the answer, and then ask the question again.

Instructor: What kind of coins did Oliver buy his ticket with?
Student: He bought his ticket with dimes.

Instructor: Why did Oliver follow so closely behind a large family?
Student: He wanted to look like he belonged to them.

Instructor: What kind of animal sound did Oliver hear as he was climbing the steps into the circus?
Student: He heard a lion roar.

Instructor: What kind of shells were crunching under his feet?
Student: Peanut shells were crunching under his feet.

Instructor: How many large caged rings were on the sawdust?
Student: There were three rings.

Instructor: Can you remember the two other kinds of animals (besides lions) that were in the nearest ring?
Student: There were bears and a leopard in the ring.

Instructor: What did the trainer make one of the bears do?
Student: The bear pushed another bear in a baby carriage.

Instructor: What did the lions do while the bear pushed the baby carriage?
Student: They sat up and begged.

Ask, "What is one thing you remember about the passage?" Write the student's answer down on the "Instructor" lines of Student Page 52 as he watches. This answer can be the same as one of the answers above.

Now ask the student to copy the sentence in pencil on the "Student" lines below the model. If the sentence is too long for comfort, he can copy only the first eight to ten words.

WEEK 14

DAY ONE: Copywork   *Student Page 53*

Focus: *Capitalizing months of the year*

Pull out Student Page 53. Write the student's name and the date for her as she watches, or ask her to write the name and date independently.

Ask the student to look at the following rhyme, which is printed on Student Page 53. Read the poem out loud as she follows along:

> Thirty days hath September,
> April, June, and November.
> All the rest have thirty-one,
> Except for February alone.
> Which has four and twenty-four,
> Til leap year gives it one day more.

Explain that there are 12 months in each year. September, April, June, and November all have 30 days; January, March, May, July, August, October, and December have 31 days. February has 28 days, but every four years, February has 29 days. The years when February has 29 days are called "leap years."

Tell the student that the names of months are **proper nouns**. Have the student point to the capital letters that begin the names of the months in the poem. Then ask the student to look at the following two model sentences, which are also printed on the Student Page:

> The month of December has 31 days.
> The months of January, March, August, and October all have 31 days.

Choose whichever sentence is appropriate to the student's handwriting ability. Watch the student as she writes in pencil. If she begins to make an error, gently stop her and ask her to look at the model again.

DAY TWO: Narration Exercise   *Student Page 54*

Pull out Student Page 54. Write the student's name and the date for her as she watches, or ask her to write the name and date independently.

Read the following poem out loud to the student. Tell her that although the poem is short, you will be asking her to explain in her own words what the child in the poem is complaining about.

In winter I get up at night
And dress by yellow candle-light.
In summer, quite the other way,
I have to go to bed by day.
I have to go to bed and see
The birds still hopping on the tree,
Or hear the grown-up people's feet
Still going past me in the street.
And does it not seem hard to you,
When all the sky is clear and blue,
And I should like so much to play,
To have to go to bed by day?

—"Bed in Summer"
by Robert Louis Stevenson

Ask the following questions. Remind the student to answer you in complete sentences. If she answers in a fragment, turn the fragment into a complete sentence, say it to her, and then ask her to repeat this sentence back to you. If she cannot answer a question, read her the part of the poem that contains the answer, and then ask the question again.

Instructor: In winter, when does the child get up?
Student: *He gets up at night.* [You may need to explain that the child is getting up in the morning, but that it is still dark because the sun rises later in the winter than in the summer.]

Instructor: In summer, when does the child go to bed?
Student: *He goes to bed during the day.* [You may need to explain that the sun sets much later in the summer than in the winter—sometimes it is still light at eight or nine PM.]

Instructor: Can you remember one of the two things that the child can see or hear when he is in bed?
Student: *He can see birds in the trees and hear feet going past.*

Instructor: What does the sky look like when the child goes to bed in the summer?
Student: *The sky is clear and blue.*

Instructor: Does the child want to go to bed?
Student: *No, the child wants to play.*

Ask, "Why is the child unhappy?" Write the student's answer down on Student Page 54 as she watches. If necessary, help her form an answer that sounds like one of the following:

"He doesn't want to go to bed while it is light outside."

"She thinks it's unfair that she has to get up when it is dark in winter and go to bed while it is light in the summer."

"He doesn't like getting up in the dark or going to bed during the day."

"She wants to get up and play at night during the summer when it's light, but she has to go to bed."

DAY THREE: Copywork   *Student Page 55*

Focus: *Capitalizing months of the year*

Pull out Student Page 55. Write the student's name and the date for her as she watches, or ask her to write the name and date independently.

The following two model sentences are already printed on it:

> June and July are summer months.
> December and January are winter months, but March is a spring month.

Ask the student to look carefully at the sentences. While she is examining the sentences, explain that we capitalize the names of the months of the year, but that we do *not* capitalize the names of the seasons—winter, spring, summer, and fall. These are not **proper nouns**, but the names of the months *are*. Ask her to point to the names June, July, December, January, and March; these are **proper nouns**. Then ask her to point to the words "summer", "winter", and "spring". These are the names of seasons (times of the year); they are not proper nouns, so they do not begin with capital letters.

Choose whichever sentence is appropriate to the student's handwriting ability. Watch the student as she writes in pencil. If she begins to make an error, gently stop her and ask her to look at the model again.

DAY FOUR: Narration Exercise and Copywork   *Student Page 56*

Pull out Student Page 56. Write the student's name and the date for her as she watches, or ask her to write the name and date independently.

Read the following story out loud to the student.

> One cold winter morning, a hungry bear was padding through the forest, leaving big bear footprints in the snow. Soon he saw a fox up ahead of him, trotting happily through the snow with a huge trout in his mouth.
>
> "Good morning!" the bear bellowed at the fox. "Where did you get that fish?"
>
> Now, the fox had stolen the fish out of the kitchen of a nearby farm. But he thought that he might as well have some fun with the huge hungry bear.
>
> "Oh, I've been out fishing in the lake," the fox said. "There are more sweet, cold trout there than you can shake a stick at."
>
> The bear felt his mouth watering at the thought. "How can I get a fish for myself?" he demanded.
>
> "Easy!" said the fox. "Tomorrow at dawn, go down to the lake, take a rock, and break a hole in the ice. Then, sit down beside the hole and let your tail hang down into the water. Make sure that you stay there all morning.

Your tail might get a bit sore, but don't pull it out—that means the fish are biting! Then, around lunch time, gather yourself together and jump up as fast as you can. Your tail will come flying out of the hole with a whole mess of fish holding on to it."

In those days the bear had a long, furry tail—and although he was hungry, he wasn't very smart. So the next morning, he went down to the lake and did as the fox said. He sat on the ice all morning with his tail hanging down into the cold, cold water. His tail grew colder and colder, and hurt more and more. But he stayed on the ice, thinking about all the fish he would catch and eat.

Finally, it was time for lunch. The bear got his big hind paws right under him and suddenly jumped sideways as fast he could. But the hole had frozen back up again. His tail was stuck hard in the ice, and when he leaped up, it snapped right off!

The bear yelped and scurried off into the woods, leaving his long tail behind him. And that's why bears have short stumpy tails, right up to the present day.

—Traditional folk tale
adapted by Susan Wise Bauer

Ask the following questions. Remind the student to answer you in complete sentences. If she answers in a fragment, turn the fragment into a complete sentence, say it to her, and then ask her to repeat this sentence back to you. If she cannot answer a question, read her the part of the passage that contains the answer, and then ask the question again.

Instructor: When the bear met the fox, what kind of fish did the fox have in his mouth?
Student: *The fox had a trout in his mouth.*

Instructor: Where did the fox get the fish?
Student: *He stole it from a farm.*

Instructor: Where did the fox *say* that he'd gotten the fish?
Student: *He said he'd gotten it out of the lake.*

Instructor: What did the fox tell the bear to do?
Student: *He told the bear to break a hole in the ice, let his tail hang through it, and not to take his tail out until lunch time. Then the bear was supposed to jump up and pull his tail out of the water.* [If the student forgets any one of these steps, remind her of it.]

Instructor: What kind of tail did the bear have?
Student: *He had a long furry tail.*

Instructor: What happened to the bear's tail while he was sitting on the ice?
Student: *It froze into the ice.*

Instructor: What happened when the bear jumped up?
Student: *His tail snapped off.*

Instructor: This story says that it explains something about bears (but the explanation is just pretend). What does the story explain?
Student: *It explains why bears have short tails.*

Ask, "What is one thing you remember about the passage?" Write the student's answer down on the "Instructor" lines of Student Page 56 as she watches. This answer can be the same as one of the answers above.

Now ask the student to copy the sentence in pencil on the "Student" lines below the model. If the sentence is too long for comfort, she can copy only the first eight to ten words.

WEEK 15

DAY ONE: Copywork   *Student Page 57*

Focus: *Capitalizing months of the year*

Pull out Student Page 57. Write the student's name and the date for him as he watches, or ask him to write the name and date independently.

The following two model sentences are already printed on it:

> But in June came three wet days.
> It was September, and the turf was dry and crisp.

Ask the student to look carefully at the sentences. While he is examining the sentences, explain that these sentences are from *The Railway Children,* by Edith Nesbit. Edith Nesbit lived in England over a hundred years ago. In *The Railway Children,* she wrote about three children who moved out to the country with their mother. The children lived beside a train track, and spent many days in the summer and in the fall exploring the outdoors. You may need to explain that turf is another name for short thick grass.

Remind the student that the names of months are **proper nouns**, so they always begin with a capital letter. Have the student point to the capital letters that begin the names June and September.

Choose whichever sentence is appropriate to the student's handwriting ability. Watch the student as he writes in pencil. If he begins to make an error, gently stop him and ask him to look at the model again.

DAY TWO: Narration Exercise   *Student Page 58*

Pull out Student Page 58. Write the student's name and the date for him as he watches, or ask him to write the name and date independently.

Explain that the following passage is from *The Railway Children*. It comes at the beginning of the book, right before the children move out to the country. They have a perfect life—but suddenly their lives change.

> There were three of them. Roberta was the eldest. Of course, mothers never have favourites, but if their mother *had* had a favourite, it might have been Roberta. Next came Peter, who wished to be an engineer when he grew up; and the youngest was Phyllis, who meant extremely well.
>
> Mother did not spend all her time in paying dull calls to dull ladies, and sitting dully at home waiting for dull ladies to pay calls to her. She was almost always there, ready to play with the children, and read to them, and help them to do their home-lessons. Besides this she used to write stories for them while they were at school, and read them aloud after tea, and she always made up funny pieces of poetry for their birthdays and for other great occasions, such as the christening of the new kittens, or the refurnishing of the doll's house, or the time when they were getting over the mumps.
>
> These three lucky children always had everything they needed: pretty clothes, good fires, a lovely nursery with heaps of toys, and a Mother Goose wall-paper. They had a kind and merry nursemaid, and a dog who was called James, and who was their very own. They also had a Father who was just perfect—never cross, never unjust, and always ready for a game—at least, if at any time he was *not* ready, he always had an excellent reason for it, and explained the reason to the children so interestingly and funnily that they felt sure he couldn't help himself.
>
> You will think that they ought to have been very happy. And so they were, but they did not know *how* happy till the pretty life in the Red Villa was over and done with, and they had to live a very different life indeed.
>
> —From *The Railway Children*
> by Edith Nesbit

Ask the following questions. Remind the student to answer you in complete sentences. If he answers in a fragment, turn the fragment into a complete sentence, say it to him, and then ask him to repeat this sentence back to you. If he cannot answer a question, read him the part of the passage that contains the answer, and then ask the question again.

Instructor: What were the names of the three children?
Student: *Their names were Roberta, Peter, and Phyllis.*

Instructor: Who was the oldest of the three?
Student: *Roberta was oldest.*

Instructor: What was Peter going to be when he grew up?
Student: *He was going to be an engineer.*

Instructor: Which child was the youngest?
Student: *Phyllis was the youngest.*

Instructor: Mother used to make up poetry on four special occasions. Can you remember two of them?

Student: *She made up poetry for birthdays, for new kittens, for refurnishing the doll's house, and for getting over the mumps.*

Instructor: Can you remember two of the four things that the lucky children had in their nursery?

Student: *They had clothes, fires, toys, and Mother Goose wallpaper.*

Instructor: What was their dog named?

Student: *Their dog was named James.*

Instructor: If their father couldn't play a game with them, what did he do?

Student: *He explained the reason why.*

Instructor: Were they happy?

Student: *Yes, they were happy.*

Ask, "What is one thing you remember about the passage?" Write the student's answer down on Student Page 58 as he watches. This answer can be the same as one of the answers above.

DAY THREE: Copywork   *Student Page 59*

Focus: *Capitalizing days of the week*

Pull out Student Page 59. Write the student's name and the date for him as he watches, or ask him to write the name and date independently.

The following two model sentences are already printed on it:

> But it happened to be a wet day and, for July, very cold.
> They had seen the blossom on the trees in the spring, and they knew where to look for wild cherries.

Ask the student to look carefully at the sentences. Tell him that these sentences are from *The Railway Children*. Ask him to point out the name of the month, and the capital letter that begins it. Remind him that "spring" is not capitalized because it is not the name of a month—it is the name of a time of year (a season).

Choose whichever sentence is appropriate to the student's handwriting ability. Watch the student as he writes in pencil. If he begins to make an error, gently stop him and ask him to look at the model again.

DAY FOUR: Narration Exercise and Copywork   *Student Page 60*

Pull out Student Page 60. Write the student's name and the date for him as he watches, or ask him to write the name and date independently.

Read the following passage out loud to the student. Explain that the happy life of the three children has suddenly changed. They don't know what's happened—but their father has had to go away, and their mother suddenly tells them that they must give up their house and go live in the country instead. So they pack up all of their clothes and toys, and get on a train so that they can travel to their new home.

At first they enjoyed looking out of the window, but when it grew dusk they grew sleepier and sleepier, and no one knew how long they had been in the train when they were roused by Mother's shaking them gently and saying, "Wake up, dears. We're there."

They woke up, cold and melancholy, and stood shivering on the drafty platform while the baggage was taken out of the train. Then the engine, puffing and blowing, set to work again, and dragged the train away. The children watched the tail-lights of the guard's van disappear into the darkness.

This was the first train the children saw on that railway which was in time to become so very dear to them. They did not guess then how they would grow to love the railway, and how soon it would become the center of their new life, nor what wonders and changes it would bring to them. They only shivered and sneezed and hoped the walk to the new house would not be long. Peter's nose was colder than he ever remembered it to have been before. Roberta's hat was crooked, and the elastic seemed tighter than usual. Phyllis's shoe-laces had come undone.

"Come," said Mother, "we've got to walk. There aren't any cabs here."

The walk was dark and muddy. The children stumbled a little on the rough road, and once Phyllis absently fell into a puddle, and was picked up damp and unhappy. There were no gas-lamps on the road, and the road was uphill. The cart went at a foot's pace, and they followed the gritty crunch of its wheels. As their eyes got used to the darkness, they could see the mound of boxes swaying dimly in front of them.

A long gate had to be opened for the cart to pass through, and after that the road seemed to go across fields—and now it went down hill. Presently a great dark lumpish thing showed over to the right.

"There's the house," said Mother.

—From *The Railway Children*
by Edith Nesbit

Ask the following questions. Remind the student to answer you in complete sentences. If he answers in a fragment, turn the fragment into a complete sentence, say it to him, and then ask him to repeat this sentence back to you. If he cannot answer a question, read him the part of the passage that contains the answer, and then ask the question again.

Instructor: Did the children stay awake for the whole train journey?
Student: *No, they fell asleep.*

Instructor: When they got off the train, each one of the three children had a different problem. Can you remember two of the problems?
Student: *Peter's nose was cold, Roberta's hat was crooked and tight, and Phyllis's shoe laces were untied.*

Instructor: How did they get from the train station to the new house?
Student: *They walked.*

Instructor: What happened to Phyllis?
Student: *She fell in a puddle.*

Instructor: Can you remember what the house looked like when they first saw it?
Student: *They saw a great dark lumpish thing.*

Ask, "What is one thing you remember about the passage?" Write the student's answer down on the "Instructor" lines of Student Page 60 as he watches. This answer can be the same as one of the answers above.

Now ask the student to copy the sentence in pencil on the "Student" lines below the model. If the sentence is too long for comfort, he can copy only the first eight to ten words.

WEEK 16

DAY ONE: Copywork   *Student Page 61*

Focus: *Capitalizing days of the week and months of the year*

Pull out Student Page 61. Write the student's name and the date for her as she watches, or ask her to write the name and date independently.

The following model sentences are already printed on it:

Today is _____, _____ _____, _____.
               (day of the week)   (month)   (day)   (year)

I was born on _____, _____ _____, _____.
                (day of the week)   (month)   (day)   (year)

As the student watches, write the appropriate day of the week, the month, the day of the month, and the year in each blank. Ask the student to point to the capital letters that begin the name of the day of the week and the name of the month. Remind her that these are **proper nouns**.

Depending on the student's handwriting ability, ask her to copy one or both of the sentences. Watch the student as she writes in pencil. If she begins to make an error, gently stop her and ask her to look at the model again.

Note: At the webpage www.timeanddate.com/calendar/, you can create a calendar for the child's year of birth which will show the day of the week on which she was born.

DAY TWO: Narration Exercise   *Student Page 62*

Pull out Student Page 62. Write the student's name and the date for her as she watches, or ask her to write the name and date independently.

Read the following story out loud. Try to use different voices for the girl and the old gentleman.

> A girl once went to the fair to hire herself for a servant. At last a funny-looking old gentleman hired her, and took her home to his house. When she got there, he told her that he had something to teach her, because in his house he had his own names for things.
>
> He said to her, "What will you call me?"
>
> "Master or mister, or whatever you please, sir," said she.
>
> He said, "You must call me 'Master of all Masters.' And what would you call this?" pointing to his bed.
>
> She said, "Bed or couch, or whatever you please, sir."
>
> "No, that's my 'barnacle.' And what do you call these?" said he, pointing to his pants.
>
> She said, "Pants or trousers, or whatever you please, sir."
>
> "You must call them 'squibs and crackers,'" he said. "And what would you call her?" pointing to the cat.
>
> "Cat or kitty, or whatever you please, sir," she said.
>
> He said, "You must call her 'white-faced simminy.' And this, now," showing the fire, "what would you call this?"
>
> "Fire or flame, or whatever you please, sir," said she.
>
> "You must call it 'hot cockalorum.' And what would you call this?" he went on, pointing to the water.
>
> "Water or wetness, or whatever you please, sir," said she.
>
> "No, 'pondalorum' is its name. And what do you call all this?" asked he, as he pointed to the house.
>
> "House or cottage, or whatever you please, sir," said she.
>
> "You must call it 'high topper mountain,'" he told her.
>
> That very night the servant woke her master up in a fright and said: "Master of all Masters, get out of your barnacle and put on your squibs and crackers. For white-faced simminy has got a spark of hot cockalorum on its tail, and unless you get some pondalorum, high topper mountain will be all on hot cockalorum."

—"Master of All Masters"
folk tale retold by Joseph Jacobs

Ask the following questions. Remind the student to answer you in complete sentences. If she answers in a fragment, turn the fragment into a complete sentence, say it to her, and then ask her to repeat this sentence back to you. If she cannot answer a question, read her the part of the passage that contains the answer, and then ask the question again.

Instructor: What did the girl have to call the old man?
Student: *She had to call him "Master of All Masters."*

Instructor: Do you remember what the "barnacle" was?
Student: *The barnacle was his bed.*

Instructor: What did the old man call his pants?
Student: *He called them "squibs and crackers."*

Instructor: What was the "white-face simminy?"
Student: *It was the cat.*

Instructor: What did the old man call the fire?
Student: *He called it "hot cockalorum."*

Instructor: What was the "pondalorum?"
Student: *It was the water.*

Instructor: What did the old man call the house?
Student: *He called it the "high topper mountain."*

Instructor: What did the girl mean when she said, "Get out of your barnacle and put on your squibs and crackers"?
Student: *She meant, "Get out of bed and put on your pants."*

Instructor: Can you say "The cat has got a spark of fire on its tail" in the old man's silly language?
Student: *"The white-faced simminy has got a spark of hot cockalorum on its tail."*

Instructor: What did the girl mean when she said, "Unless you get some pondalorum, high topper mountain will be all on hot cockalorum?"
Student: *She meant, "Unless you get some water, the house will be all on fire."*

Ask, "What is one thing you remember about the passage?" Write the student's answer down on Student Page 62 as she watches. This answer can be the same as one of the answers above.

DAY THREE: Copywork   *Student Page 63*

Focus: *Capitalizing names of places*

Pull out Student Page 63. Write the student's name and the date for her as she watches, or ask her to write the name and date independently.

The following two model sentences are already printed on it:

> Aesop was a slave who lived in ancient Greece.
> Aesop lived on an island called Samos. He once visited Athens, the greatest city in Greece.

Ask the student to look carefully at the sentences. Tell her that these sentences are about the Greek slave Aesop, who lived around 550 BC—twenty-five hundred years ago. We don't know very much about the life of Aesop, but we think that he wrote a number of stories that still survive today. The stories are about animals—but each story teaches a lesson about the way *people* should behave.

Ask the student to point to the capital letters that begin the names Greece, Samos, and Athens. Remind her that she has already learned to capitalize the names of cities, towns, and states. We also capitalize the names of countries, like Greece, and particular places, like Samos. Samos is the name of one particular island.

Choose whichever sentence is appropriate to the student's handwriting ability. Watch the student as she writes in pencil. If she begins to make an error, gently stop her and ask her to look at the model again.

DAY FOUR: Narration Exercise and Copywork   *Student Page 64*

Pull out Student Page 64. Write the student's name and the date for her as she watches, or ask her to write the name and date independently.

Read the following passage out loud to the student. Explain that this is one of Aesop's "fables"—one of his stories about the way people should act. Tell the student to listen for the "moral" at the end of the story—the sentence that explains what the story means.

> A dog, to whom the butcher had thrown a bone, was hurrying home with his prize as fast as he could go.
>
> As he crossed a narrow footbridge, he happened to look down and saw himself reflected in the quiet water as if in a mirror. But the greedy dog thought he saw a real dog carrying a bone much bigger than his own.
>
> If he had stopped to think he would have known better. But instead of thinking, he dropped his bone and sprang at the dog in the river, only to find himself swimming for dear life to reach the shore. At last he managed to scramble out, and as he stood sadly thinking about the good bone he had lost, he realized what a stupid dog he had been.
>
> **Moral:** If you are too greedy, you may lose even what you already have.

> —From "The Dog and His Reflection"
> by Aesop

Ask the following questions. Remind the student to answer you in complete sentences. If she answers in a fragment, turn the fragment into a complete sentence, say it to her, and then ask her to repeat this sentence back to you. If she cannot answer a question, read her the part of the passage that contains the answer, and then ask the question again.

Instructor: What did the dog have in his mouth?
Student: He had a bone in his mouth.

Instructor: What did he see when he looked in the water?
Student: He saw himself in the water OR He saw another dog.

Instructor: Why did he want that dog's bone?
Student: That bone looked bigger than his bone.

Instructor: What did the dog do?
Student: He jumped into the water.

Instructor: Did he find another dog?
Student: No, he did not.

Instructor: What happened to his bone?
Student: His bone fell into the water and he lost it.

Instructor: What might happen if you are too greedy?
Student: You might lose what you already have.

Ask, "What is one thing you remember about the passage?" Write the student's answer down on the "Instructor" lines of Student Page 64 as she watches. This answer can be the same as one of the answers above.

Now ask the student to copy the sentence in pencil on the "Student" lines below the model. If the sentence is too long for comfort, she can copy only the first eight to ten words.

WEEK 17

DAY ONE: Copywork   *Student Page 65*

Focus: *Capitalizing "I" in the middle of a sentence*

Pull out Student Page 65. Write the student's name and the date for him as he watches, or ask him to write the name and date independently.

The following two model sentences are already printed on it:

You know about sheep, and I know about dragons.
I always said, you know, that that cave up there was a dragon-cave.

Ask the student to look carefully at the sentences. While he is examining the sentences, explain that these sentences are from a book called *The Reluctant Dragon,* by Kenneth Grahame. In the next lesson, you will read a passage from *The Reluctant Dragon.*

Explain that "I" is a pronoun because it stands for a noun—your name! Whenever you use the pronoun "I," it is always capitalized. Have the student point to the "I" in the middle of the first sentence.

Choose whichever sentence is appropriate to the student's handwriting ability. Watch the student as he writes in pencil. If he begins to make an error, gently stop him and ask him to look at the model again.

DAY TWO: Narration Exercise   *Student Page 66*

Pull out Student Page 66. Write the student's name and the date for him as he watches, or ask him to write the name and date independently.

Read the following passage to the student. In this selection from *The Reluctant Dragon,* a shepherd is telling his wife and son that he's been hearing odd noises while watching out for the sheep. You may need to explain that to "take a cast around" is an old-fashioned way of saying "looking around."

"It began some nights ago," said the shepherd. "You know that cave up there—I never liked it, somehow, and the sheep never liked it neither, and when sheep don't like a thing there's generally some reason for it. Well, for some time past there's been faint noises coming from that cave—noises like heavy sighings, with grunts mixed up in them; and sometimes a snoring, far away down—real snoring, yet somehow not honest snoring, like you and me 'nights, you know!"

"*I* know," remarked the Boy quietly.

"Of course I was terrible frightened," the shepherd went on; "yet somehow I couldn't keep away. So this very evening, before I come down, I took a cast round by the cave, quietly. And there—O lord there I saw at last, as plain as I see you!"

"Saw *who*?" said his wife, beginning to share her husband's nervous terror!

"Why *him*, I'm a-telling you!" said the shepherd. "He was sticking half-way out of the cave and seemed to be enjoying of the cool of the evening in a poetical sort of way. He was as big as four cart-horses, and all covered with shiny scales—deep-blue scales at the top of him, shading off to a tender sort o' green below. As he breathed, there was that sort of flicker over his nostrils that you see over our chalk roads on a baking windless day in summer. He had his chin on his paws, and I should say he was meditating about things. Oh, yes, a peaceable sort o' beast enough, and not ramping or carrying on or doing anything but what was quite right and proper. I admit all that. And yet, what am I to do? Scales, you know, and claws, and a tail for certain,

> though I didn't see that end of him—I ain't used to 'em, and I don't hold with 'em, and that's a fact!"
>
> The Boy, who had apparently been absorbed in his book during his father's recital, now closed the volume, yawned, clasped his hands behind his head, and said sleepily:
>
> "It's all right, father. Don't you worry. It's only a dragon."
>
> —From *The Reluctant Dragon*
> by Kenneth Grahame

Ask the following questions. Remind the student to answer you in complete sentences. If he answers in a fragment, turn the fragment into a complete sentence, say it to him, and then ask him to repeat this sentence back to you. If he cannot answer a question, read him the part of the passage that contains the answer, and then ask the question again.

Instructor: What did the shepherd hear coming from the cave?
Student: *He heard faint noises, like heavy sighings, grunts, and snorings.*

Instructor: How did the sheep feel about the cave?
Student: *They didn't like it!*

Instructor: What did the shepherd finally decide to do about the noises?
Student: *He decided to take a look around the cave.*

Instructor: What did he see in the cave?
Student: *He saw a dragon!*

Instructor: How big was the dragon?
Student: *The dragon was as big as four horses.*

Instructor: What two colors were his scales?
Student: *The scales were blue and green.*

Instructor: What was the boy doing while his father talked?
Student: *He was reading a book.*

Ask, "What is one thing you remember about the passage?" Write the student's answer down on Student Page 66 as he watches. This answer can be the same as one of the answers above.

DAY THREE: Copywork   *Student Page 67*

Focus: *Capitalizing "I" in the middle of a sentence*

Pull out Student Page 67. Write the student's name and the date for him as he watches, or ask him to write the name and date independently.

The following model sentences are already printed on it:

You must tell him that I will not fight.
In the old days, I always let the other dragons do all the fighting.

Ask the student to look carefully at the sentences. While he is examining the sentences, explain that these are sentences that the dragon says in *The Reluctant Dragon*. In the story, the boy goes up to the cave and meets the dragon. He is a very peaceful dragon; instead of fighting, he likes to write poetry.

Remind the student that the pronoun "I" is always capitalized. Have the student point to the "I" in the middle of each sentence.

Choose whichever sentence is appropriate to the student's handwriting ability. Watch the student as he writes in pencil. If he begins to make an error, gently stop him and ask him to look at the model again.

Day Four: Narration Exercise and Copywork   *Student Page 68*

Pull out Student Page 68. Write the student's name and the date for him as he watches, or ask him to write the name and date independently.

Read the following passage out loud to the student. Explain that, even though the dragon is peaceful, the villagers send a message to the great dragon-slayer Saint George, asking him to come and slay their dragon. When Saint George comes, the boy takes him up to the cave so that he and the dragon can figure out how to avoid a fight.

"So glad to meet you, St. George," began the dragon rather nervously, "because you've been a great traveller, I hear, and I've always been rather a stay-at-home. But I can show you many antiquities, many interesting features of our country-side, if you're stopping here any time—"

"I think," said St. George, in his frank, pleasant way, "that we'd really better take the advice of our young friend here, and try to come to some understanding, on a business footing, about this little affair of ours. Now don't you think that after all the simplest plan would be just to fight it out, according to the rules, and let the best man win? They're betting on you, I may tell you, down in the village, but I don't mind that!"

"Oh, yes, do, dragon," said the Boy, delightedly; "it'll save such a lot of bother!"

"My young friend, you shut up," said the dragon severely. "Believe me, St. George," he went on, "there's nobody in the world I'd sooner oblige than you and this young gentleman here. But….there's absolutely nothing to fight about, from beginning to end. And anyhow I'm not going to, so that settles it!"

"But supposing I make you?" said St. George, rather nettled.

"You can't," said the dragon, triumphantly. "I should only go into my cave and retire for a time down the hole I came up. You'd soon get heartily sick of sitting outside and waiting for me to come out and fight you. And as soon as you'd really gone away, why, I'd come up again gaily, for I tell you frankly, I like this place, and I'm going to stay here!"

St. George gazed for a while on the fair landscape around them. "But this would be a beautiful place for a fight," he began again persuasively. "These great bare rolling Downs for the arena,—and me in my golden armour showing up against your big blue scaly coils! Think what a picture it would make!"

"Now you're trying to get at me through my artistic sensibilities," said the dragon. "But it won't work. Not but what it would make a very pretty picture, as you say," he added, wavering a little.

"We seem to be getting rather nearer to business," put in the Boy. "You must see, dragon, that there's got to be a fight of some sort, 'cos you can't want to have to go down that dirty old hole again and stop there till goodness knows when."

"It might be arranged," said St. George, thoughtfully. "I must spear you somewhere, of course, but I'm not bound to hurt you very much. There's such a lot of you that there must be a few spare places somewhere. Here, for instance, just behind your foreleg. It couldn't hurt you much, just here!"

"Now you're tickling, George," said the dragon, coyly. "No, that place won't do at all. Even if it didn't hurt,—and I'm sure it would, awfully,—it would make me laugh, and that would spoil everything."

"Let's try somewhere else, then," said St. George, patiently. "Under your neck, for instance,—all these folds of thick skin,—if I speared you here you'd never even know I'd done it!"

"Yes, but are you sure you can hit off the right place?" asked the dragon, anxiously.

"Of course I am," said St. George, with confidence. "You leave that to me!"

—From *The Reluctant Dragon*
by Kenneth Grahame

Ask the following questions. Remind the student to answer you in complete sentences. If he answers in a fragment, turn the fragment into a complete sentence, say it to him, and then ask him to repeat this sentence back to you. If he cannot answer a question, read him the part of the passage that contains the answer, and then ask the question again.

Instructor: When St. George goes to see the dragon, what does he first suggest that he and the dragon should do?
Student: *He suggests that they have a fight.*

Instructor: Does the dragon agree to fight?
Student: *No, he does not.*

Instructor: When St. George says that he'll make the dragon fight, what does the dragon say that he'll do instead?
Student: *He says that he'll go down into his cave.*

Instructor: What is the next thing that St. George says, as he tries to convince the dragon to fight?
Student: *He says that the fight would make a beautiful picture.*

Instructor: What is St. George's final suggestion about the fight?
Student: *He says that he could spear the dragon without hurting him.*

Instructor: What two places does he suggest spearing the dragon?
Student: *He says he can spear the dragon behind the foreleg or under the neck.*

Ask, "What is one thing you remember about the passage?" Write the student's answer down on the "Instructor" lines of Student Page 68 as he watches. This answer can be the same as one of the answers above.

Now ask the student to copy the sentence in pencil on the "Student" lines below the model. If the sentence is too long for comfort, he can copy only the first eight to ten words.

WEEK 18

DAY ONE: Copywork   *Student Page 69*

Focus: *Pronouns*

Pull out Student Page 69. Write the student's name and the date for her as she watches, or ask her to write the name and date independently.

The following two model sentences are already printed on it:

> It was a warm day, and he had a long way to go.
> Outside his house he found Piglet, jumping up and down trying to reach the knocker.

Ask the student to look carefully at the sentences. While she is examining the sentences, explain to the student that these sentences are from *Winnie-the-Pooh,* by A. A. Milne. Tell the student to point to the word "he" in the first sentence. "He" stands for the name "Winnie the Pooh." Because "he" is used in the place of a noun (name), it is a pronoun. It begins with a small letter, not a capital letter, because pronouns other than I are not capitalized. Ask the student to point to the word "his" in the second sentence. This is also a pronoun. The other way to write this sentence would be, "Outside Winnie-the-Pooh's house, Winnie-the-Pooh found Piglet." "His" takes the place of the proper noun "Winnie the Pooh."

Choose whichever sentence is appropriate to the student's handwriting ability. Watch the student as she writes in pencil. If she begins to make an error, gently stop her and ask her to look at the model again.

DAY TWO: Narration Exercise   *Student Page 70*

Pull out Student Page 70. Write the student's name and the date for her as she watches, or ask her to write the name and date independently.

Tell the student that Pooh has decided to take Eeyore a jar of honey for his birthday. He is hurrying back to give Eeyore the present, when he starts to feel hungry.

If the student is looking on and asks about the capitalization of "Useful," tell her that A. A. Milne, the writer, was pretending to be Pooh in that sentence, and that Pooh doesn't know how to capitalize properly.

> It was a warm day, and he had a long way to go. He hadn't gone more than half-way when a sort of funny feeling began to creep all over him. It began at the tip of his nose and trickled all through him and out at the soles of his feet. It was just as if somebody inside him were saying, "Now then, Pooh, time for a little something."
>
> "Dear, dear," said Pooh, "I didn't know it was as late as that." So he sat down and took the top off his jar of honey. "Lucky I brought this with me," he thought. "Many a bear going out on a warm day like this would never have thought to bring a little something with him." And he began to eat.
>
> "Now let me see," he thought, as he took his last lick of the inside of the jar, "where was I going? Ah, yes, Eeyore." He got up slowly.
>
> And then, suddenly, he remembered. He had eaten Eeyore's birthday present!
>
> "*Bother!*" said Pooh. "What *shall* I do? I *must* give him *something.*"
>
> For a little while he couldn't think of anything. Then he thought: "Well, it's a very nice pot, even if there's no honey in it, and if I washed it clean, and got somebody to write '*A Happy Birthday*' on it, Eeyore could keep things in it, which might be Useful."

> —From *Winnie-the-Pooh*
> by A. A. Milne

Ask the following questions. Remind the student to answer you in complete sentences. If she answers in a fragment, turn the fragment into a complete sentence, say it to her, and then ask her to repeat this sentence back to you. If she cannot answer a question, read her the part of the passage that contains the answer, and then ask the question again.

Instructor: How did Pooh know that he was hungry?
Student: *He had a funny feeling OR He felt like it was time for a little something.*

Instructor: What did he do when he felt hungry?
Student: *He started to eat the honey.*

Instructor: After he had eaten the honey, what did he remember?
Student: *He remembered that it was Eeyore's birthday present.*

Instructor: What did he decide to do with the pot?
Student: *He decided to wash it out and give it to Eeyore anyway.*

Instructor: What did Pooh want to write on the pot?
Student: *He wanted to write "A Happy Birthday."*

Ask, "What is one thing you remember about the passage?" Write the student's answer down on Student Page 70 as she watches. This answer can be the same as one of the answers above.

DAY THREE: Copywork

Student Page 71

Focus: *Other pronouns*

Pull out Student Page 71. Write the student's name and the date for her as she watches, or ask her to write the name and date independently.

The following model sentences are already printed on it:

> He dropped his pine cone into the river.
> But then he thought he would just look at the river instead, because it was a peaceful sort of day.

Ask the student to look carefully at the sentences. While she is examining the sentences, tell her that the sentences are about Winnie-the-Pooh. You will read the story that these sentences come from in the next lesson. Remind her that pronouns are words that take the place of nouns. The pronoun "I" is the only pronoun that is capitalized.

Ask the student to point to the three places where the pronoun "he" refers to Winnie-the-Pooh. Then ask her to point to the pronoun "it" in the second sentence. This pronoun refers to the beautiful day. Ask the student why the first "He" is capitalized (it is the first word in the sentence).

Choose whichever sentence is appropriate to the student's handwriting ability. Watch the student as she writes in pencil. If she begins to make an error, gently stop her and ask her to look at the model again.

DAY FOUR: Narration Exercise and Copywork

Student Page 72

Pull out Student Page 72. Write the student's name and the date for her as she watches, or ask her to write the name and date independently.

Tell the student that the following story comes from "Eeyore Joins a Game," by A. A. Milne. Pooh was walking over the bridge in the Hundred Acre Wood, trying to make up a poem about the fir-cone (pine cone) he was carrying, when he accidentally dropped it into the water. Suggest that the student listen for the place in the story where the narrator (the person telling the story) gets confused, and raise her hand when she hears it.

> "Bother," said Pooh, as it floated slowly under the bridge, and he went back to get another fir-cone which had a rhyme to it. But then he thought he would just look at the river instead, because it was a peaceful sort of day, so

he lay down and looked at it, and it slipped slowly away beneath him...and suddenly, there was his fir-cone slipping away too.

"That's funny," said Pooh. "I dropped it on the other side," said Pooh, "and it came out on this side! I wonder if it would do it again?" And he went back for some more fir-cones.

It did. It kept on doing it. Then he dropped two in at once, and leant over the bridge to see which of them would come out first; and one of them did; but as they were both the same size, he didn't know if it was the one which he wanted to win, or the other one. So the next time he dropped one big one and one little one, and the big one came out first, which was what he had said it would do, and the little one came out last, which was what he had said it would do, so he had won twice...and when he went home for tea, he had won thirty-six and lost twenty-eight, which meant that he was—that he had—well, you take twenty-eight from thirty-six, and *that's* what he was. Instead of the other way round.

And that was the beginning of the game called Poohsticks, which Pooh invented, and which he and his friends used to play on the edge of the Forest. But they played with sticks instead of fir-cones, because they were easier to mark.

—From *The House at Pooh Corner*
by A. A. Milne

Ask the following questions. Remind the student to answer you in complete sentences. If she answers in a fragment, turn the fragment into a complete sentence, say it to her, and then ask her to repeat this sentence back to you. If she cannot answer a question, read her the part of the passage that contains the answer, and then ask the question again.

Instructor: What did Pooh say when he dropped his fir-cone?
Student: He said "Bother."

Instructor: What did he do then?
Student: He lay down on the bridge to watch the river.

Instructor: What did he see then?
Student: He saw his fir-cone floating out from under the bridge.

Instructor: What did Pooh call the game he invented?
Student: He called it Poohsticks.

Instructor: Did Pooh and his friends play the game with fir-cones?
Student: No, they played with sticks.

Ask, "What is one thing you remember about the passage?" Write the student's answer down on the "Instructor" lines of Student Page 72 as she watches. This answer can be the same as one of the answers above.

Now ask the student to copy the sentence in pencil on the "Student" lines below the model. If the sentence is too long for comfort, she can copy only the first eight to ten words.

WEEK 19

DAY ONE: Copywork

Focus: *Pronouns*

Pull out Student Page 73. Write the student's name and the date for him as he watches, or ask him to write the name and date independently.

The following two model sentences are already printed on it:

> When she was angry, her little eyes flashed blue.
> The wrinkles of contempt crossed the wrinkles of peevishness, and made her face as full of wrinkles as a pat of butter.

Ask the student to look carefully at the sentences. While he is examining the sentences, explain to the student that these sentences are from *The Light Princess,* by George MacDonald. This story is a little like "Sleeping Beauty," and these sentences describe the evil fairy who isn't invited to the celebration of the baby's birth.

Tell the student to point out the three pronouns that refer to the evil fairy: "she" and "her" in the first sentence, and "her" in the second sentence. These pronouns stand for the evil fairy's name. They are not capitalized.

Choose whichever sentence is appropriate to the student's handwriting ability. Watch the student as he writes in pencil. If he begins to make an error, gently stop him and ask him to look at the model again.

DAY TWO: Narration Exercise

Pull out Student Page 74. Write the student's name and the date for him as he watches, or ask him to write the name and date independently.

Explain that the following passage is from the beginning of *The Light Princess,* by George MacDonald. The king and queen have a daughter—and forget to invite the evil fairy, the Princess Makemnoit, to the christening. You may need to explain that "demeanour" refers to the way that someone behaves.

> The day drew near when the infant must be christened. The king wrote all the invitations with his own hand. Of course somebody was forgotten.
> Now it does not generally matter if somebody is forgotten, only you must mind who. Unfortunately, the king forgot without intending to forget; and so the chance fell upon the Princess Makemnoit, which was awkward. For the princess was the king's own sister; and he ought not to have forgotten her. But she had made herself so disagreeable to the old king, their father, that he had forgotten her in making his will; and so it was no wonder that her brother forgot her in writing his invitations. But poor relations don't do

anything to keep you in mind of them. Why don't they? The king could not see into the garret she lived in, could he?

She was a sour, spiteful creature. The wrinkles of contempt crossed the wrinkles of peevishness, and made her face as full of wrinkles as a pat of butter. If ever a king could be justified in forgetting anybody, this king was justified in forgetting his sister, even at a christening. She looked very odd, too. Her forehead was as large as all the rest of her face, and projected over it like a precipice. When she was angry, her little eyes flashed blue. When she hated anybody, they shone yellow and green. What they looked like when she loved anybody, I do not know; for I never heard of her loving anybody but herself, and I do not think she could have managed that if she had not somehow got used to herself. But what made it highly imprudent in the king to forget her was that she was awfully clever. In fact, she was a witch; and when she bewitched anybody, he very soon had enough of it; for she beat all the wicked fairies in wickedness, and all the clever ones in cleverness. She despised all the modes we read of in history, in which offended fairies and witches have taken their revenges; and therefore, after waiting and waiting in vain for an invitation, she made up her mind at last to go without one, and make the whole family miserable, like a princess as she was.

So she put on her best gown, went to the palace, was kindly received by the happy monarch, who forgot that he had forgotten her, and took her place in the procession to the royal chapel. When they were all gathered about the font, she contrived to get next to it, and throw something into the water; after which she maintained a very respectful demeanour till the water was applied to the child's face.

—From *The Light Princess*
by George MacDonald

Ask the following questions. Remind the student to answer you in complete sentences. If he answers in a fragment, turn the fragment into a complete sentence, say it to him, and then ask him to repeat this sentence back to you. If he cannot answer a question, read him the part of the passage that contains the answer, and then ask the question again.

Instructor: A baby princess was born to the king and queen. To what event did the king write out many invitations?
Student: *He wrote invitations to the baby's christening.*

Instructor: The king forgot one invitation. Whose invitation did he forget?
Student: *He forgot Princess Makemnoit OR He forgot his sister.*

Instructor: Her face was as wrinkled as a kind of food. Do you remember the food that Princess Makemnoit's face was compared to?
Student: *Her face was as wrinkled as a pat of butter.*

Instructor: Can you remember two other things about the way Princess Makemnoit looked?

Student: *She had a large forehead. Her eyes flashed blue when she was mad, and yellow and green when she hated anyone.*

Instructor: What did Princess Makemnoit decide to do when she did not receive an invitation?
Student: *She decided to go to the christening anyway.*

Instructor: What did she do to the water?
Student: *She threw something into it.*

Ask, "What is one thing you remember about the passage?" Write the student's answer down on Student Page 74 as he watches. This answer can be the same as one of the answers above.

DAY THREE: Copywork

Student Page 75

Focus: *Pronouns*

Pull out Student Page 75. Write the student's name and the date for him as he watches, or ask him to write the name and date independently.

The following model sentences are already printed on it:

> They soon found out that the princess was missing.
> The wind carried her off through the opposite window and away.

Ask the student to look carefully at the sentences. While he is examining the sentences, explain to the student that Princess Makemnoit placed a spell on the baby that made her laugh, so that she could never take anything seriously. The spell also made the baby lose her gravity. If her parents were not careful to hold onto her, she would float way.

Tell the student to point to the word "they" in the first sentence. This pronoun refers to a group of people—in this case, the king and the queen and the palace servants. Ask the student to find the pronoun that refers to the baby in the second sentence ("her").

Choose whichever sentence is appropriate to the student's handwriting ability. Watch the student as he writes in pencil. If he begins to make an error, gently stop him and ask him to look at the model again.

DAY FOUR: Narration Exercise and Copywork

Student Page 76

Pull out Student Page 76. Write the student's name and the date for him as he watches, or ask him to write the name and date independently.

Read the following passage out loud to the student.

> One fine summer day, a month after her first adventures, during which time she had been very carefully watched, the princess was lying on the bed

in the queen's own chamber, fast asleep. One of the windows was open, for it was noon, and the day was so sultry that the little girl was wrapped in nothing less ethereal than slumber itself. The queen came into the room, and not observing that the baby was on the bed, opened another window. A frolicsome fairy wind, which had been watching for a chance of mischief, rushed in at the one window, and taking its way over the bed where the child was lying, caught her up, and rolling and floating her along like a piece of flue, or a dandelion seed, carried her with it through the opposite window, and away. The queen went down-stairs, quite ignorant of the loss she had herself occasioned.

When the nurse returned, she supposed that her Majesty had carried her off, and, dreading a scolding, delayed making inquiry about her. But hearing nothing, she grew uneasy, and went at length to the queen's boudoir, where she found her Majesty.

"Please, your Majesty, shall I take the baby?" said she.

"Where is she?" asked the queen.

"Please forgive me. I know it was wrong."

"What do you mean?" said the queen, looking grave.

"Oh! don't frighten me, your Majesty!" exclaimed the nurse, clasping her hands.

The queen saw that something was amiss, and fell down in a faint. The nurse rushed about the palace, screaming, "My baby! my baby!"

Every one ran to the queen's room. But the queen could give no orders. They soon found out, however, that the princess was missing, and in a moment the palace was like a beehive in a garden; and in one minute more the queen was brought to herself by a great shout and a clapping of hands. They had found the princess fast asleep under a rose-bush, to which the elvish little wind-puff had carried her, finishing its mischief by shaking a shower of red rose-leaves all over the little white sleeper. Startled by the noise the servants made, she woke, and, furious with glee, scattered the rose-leaves in all directions, like a shower of spray in the sunset. She was watched more carefully after this, no doubt; yet it would be endless to relate all the odd incidents resulting from this peculiarity of the young princess. But there never was a baby in a house, not to say a palace, that kept the household in such constant good humour, at least below-stairs. If it was not easy for her nurses to hold her, at least she made neither their arms nor their hearts ache. And she was so nice to play at ball with! There was positively no danger of letting her fall. They might throw her down, or knock her down, or push her down, but couldn't let her down. It is true, they might let her fly into the fire or the coal-hole, or through the window; but none of these accidents had happened as yet.

—From *The Light Princess*
by George MacDonald

Ask the following questions. Remind the student to answer you in complete sentences. If he answers in a fragment, turn the fragment into a complete sentence, say it to him, and then ask him to repeat this sentence back to you. If he cannot answer a question, read him the part of the passage that contains the answer, and then ask the question again.

Instructor: Where was the princess sleeping?
Student: *She was lying on the queen's bed.*

Instructor: How many windows in the room were open?
Student: *One window was open.*

Instructor: Who came into the room?
Student: *The queen came into the room.*

Instructor: What did the queen do when she came into the room?
Student: *The queen opened another window.*

Instructor: What happened to the baby when the queen opened the second window?
Student: *The wind carried the baby out the window, and away.*

Instructor: Where did the servants find the princess?
Student: *They found her asleep under a rose-bush.*

Instructor: What did the princess do when she woke up?
Student: *She laughed and scattered the rose leaves in all directions.*

Instructor: Why did the baby not make the nurses' arms ache?
Student: *She didn't weigh anything!*

Instructor: What game did they like to play with her?
Student: *They liked to play ball with her.*

Ask, "What is one thing you remember about the passage?" Write the student's answer down on the "Instructor" lines of Student Page 76 as he watches. This answer can be the same as one of the answers above.

Now ask the student to copy the sentence in pencil on the "Student" lines below the model. If the sentence is too long for comfort, he can copy only the first eight to ten words.

WEEK 20

DAY ONE: Copywork   *Student Page 77*

Focus: *Initials as abbreviations for proper names*

Pull out Student Page 77. Write the student's name and the date for her as she watches, or ask her to write the name and date independently.

The following two model sentences are already printed on it:

> A. A. Milne wrote stories about Piglet and Pooh.
> The writer A. A. Milne really did have a son named Christopher Robin.

Ask the student to look carefully at the sentences. While she is examining the sentences, explain that these sentences are about the author of the Winnie-the-Pooh stories. His full name was Alan Alexander Milne. We can abbreviate, or shorten, a proper name by writing the first letter of the name and putting a period after it. This kind of abbreviation is called an initial. A. A. are the initials for Alan Alexander.

Choose whichever sentence is appropriate to the student's handwriting ability. Watch the student as she writes in pencil. If she begins to make an error, gently stop her and ask her to look at the model again.

DAY TWO: Narration Exercise   *Student Page 78*

Pull out Student Page 78. Write the student's name and the date for her as she watches, or ask her to write the name and date independently. Instead of writing the student's full name, you may use initials for the student's first and middle names.

Tell the student that the following passage is from *A Child's Geography of the World*, by V. M. Hillyer. He wrote this book more than fifty years ago.

> All around the outside of the world—as you probably know—is an ocean of air that covers everything on the world as the ocean of water covers everything in the sea. What you probably don't know is that this ocean of air is wrapped only round the world—it does not fill the sky. Men and animals live in this ocean of air as fish live in the ocean of water, and if a huge giant picked you out of the air you would die just as quickly as a fish does when taken out of the sea. The air is thick near the ground but gets thinner and thinner the higher up you go off the ground. That's why airplanes can go up but a few miles high—there is not enough air to hold up the plane, for the plane must have air to rest on and for its propeller to push against, just as a boat in the water must have water to rest on and water for its propeller to push against. Or if it's a jet plane, it must have air to feed its jet motors. An airplane could not rise beyond the ocean of air and sail off into the sky where there is no air any more than a steamship on the sea could rise out of the water and sail off up into the air.
>
> There is only one thing that men can send up high enough to travel above the ocean of air. That is a rocket, which doesn't depend on air for its motor or to hold it up.....

> Some mountains are so high that their tops almost stick out of the ocean of air; at least, there is so little air covering their tops that people can't go all the way to the top unless they take along canned air to breathe.
>
> You can't see air—you may think you can, but what you see is smoke or clouds, not air. When air is moving, we call it wind. Then you can feel it when it blows your hat off, you can hear it when it bangs the shutters and whistles round the house; but no one has ever seen air itself.
>
> —From *A Child's Geography of the World*
> by V. M. Hillyer

Ask the following questions. Remind the student to answer you in complete sentences. If she answers in a fragment, turn the fragment into a complete sentence, say it to her, and then ask her to repeat this sentence back to you. If she cannot answer a question, read her the part of the passage that contains the answer, and then ask the question again.

Instructor: What kind of ocean wraps all the way around the world?
Student: *An ocean of air covers the world.*

Instructor: The air is thick near the ground. What happens as it gets higher and higher?
Student: *The air gets thinner and thinner.*

Instructor: What does an airplane need for its propeller to push against?
Student: *It must have air.*

Instructor: Why can't an airplane fly up above the "ocean of air"?
Student: *The air is too thin.*

Instructor: What is the one thing that people can send up above the ocean of air?
Student: *People can send up a rocket.*

Instructor: On very high mountains, what is the air like at the top?
Student: *The air is so thin that people can't breathe.*

Instructor: What do we call air that is moving?
Student: *We call it wind.*

Instructor: Can you see the air?
Student: *No; you can only see smoke or clouds.*

Ask, "What is one thing you remember about the passage?" Write the student's answer down on Student Page 78 as she watches. This answer can be the same as one of the answers above.

DAY THREE: Copywork

Student Page 79

Focus: Initials as abbreviations for proper names

Pull out Student Page 79. Write the student's name and the date for her as she watches, or ask her to write the name and date independently.

The following model sentences are already printed on it:

> V. M. Hillyer wrote a book about geography for children.
> V. M. Hillyer thought that children should also study maps, collect stamps, and make scrapbooks about the world.

Ask the student to look carefully at the sentences. While she is examining the sentences, explain to the student that these sentences are about the author of *A Child's Geography of the World*. Ask the student to point to the initials in Mr. Hillyer's name. Remind her that an initial is the first letter of a person's name, followed by a period. Initials are capital letters, because names begin with capital letters.

Choose whichever sentence is appropriate to the student's handwriting ability. Watch the student as she writes in pencil. If she begins to make an error, gently stop her and ask her to look at the model again.

DAY FOUR: Narration Exercise and Copywork *Student Page 80*

Pull out Student Page 80. Write the student's name and the date for her as she watches, or ask her to write the name and date independently.

Read the following passage from *A Child's Geography of the World* out loud to the student.

> The outside of the world is a crust of rock like the skin of a baked potato over the hot inside. Some of the crust that you go through first is in layers, like layers in a jelly-cake, one layer after another, only these rock layers look as if they were made of sand and shells, or coal or little stones, and that's what they *are* made of....
>
> Between some of the layers of rock there is coal like jelly in a jelly-cake and in other places there are gold and silver and diamonds and rubies, and in some of the rock there are pools of oil. That's why men dig wells down through these layers of rock to get oil, and that's why men dig mines to get coal and gold.
>
> And still farther down the rock is not layers—it is just solid rock; and still farther down it gets hotter and hotter where the world has not cooled off even yet, until the rock is no longer solid, but melted.
>
> Whenever you see a chimney you know there is a furnace beneath it, and when smoke and fire come out of its top you know there is a fire in the furnace. Well, there are many places in the world where fire and smoke come out of the ground as if through a chimney from a fiery furnace. These places are called volcanoes.

> —From *A Child's Geography of the World*
> by V. M. Hillyer

Ask the following questions. Remind the student to answer you in complete sentences. If she answers in a fragment, turn the fragment into a complete sentence, say it to her, and then ask her to repeat this sentence back to you. If she cannot answer a question, read her the part of the passage that contains the answer, and then ask the question again.

Instructor: What is the crust on the outside of the world made of?
Student: *The crust is made of rock.*

Instructor: Can you name two of the four common things that the rock layers are made out of?
Student: *The layers are made out of sand, shells, coal, and little stones.*

Instructor: Can you name two of the four valuable things that sometimes lie between the layers?
Student: *Gold, silver, diamonds, and rubies lie between the layers.*

Instructor: What kinds of pools lie in some of the rock?
Student: *Pools of oil lie in some of the rock.*

Instructor: What do people dig to get the oil out?
Student: *They dig wells.*

Instructor: What do people dig to get the coal and gold out?
Student: *They dig mines.*

Instructor: What is the rock like far, far down at the center of the earth?
Student: *It is melted because it is so hot.*

Instructor: What do we call the places where fire and smoke come out of the ground?
Student: *We call them volcanoes.*

Ask, "What is one thing you remember about the passage?" Write the student's answer down on the "Instructor" lines of Student Page 80 as she watches. This answer can be the same as one of the answers above.

Now ask the student to copy the sentence in pencil on the "Student" lines below the model. If the sentence is too long for comfort, she can copy only the first eight to ten words.

WEEK 21

DAY ONE: Copywork   *Student Page 81*

Focus: *Initials as abbreviations for proper names*

Pull out Student Page 81. Write the student's name and the date for him as he watches, or ask him to write the name and date independently.

The following model sentences are already printed on it:

My full name is _____ _____ _____.
                         (first name)   (middle name)   (last name)

My initials are _____ _____ _____.
                 (first initial)   (middle initial)   (last initial)

My parent's full name is _____ _____ _____.
                                 (first name)   (middle name)   (last name)

My parent's initials are _____ _____ _____.
                        (first initial)   (middle initial)   (last initial)

As the student watches, write his name and initials and the name and initials of his mother or father in blanks. Depending on the student's handwriting ability, ask him to copy either the first two or all four of the sentences.

Choose whichever sentence is appropriate to the student's handwriting ability. Watch the student as he writes in pencil. If he begins to make an error, gently stop him and ask him to look at the model again. If necessary, remind him that each initial should have a period following it.

DAY TWO: Narration Exercise   *Student Page 82*

Pull out Student Page 82. Write the student's name and the date for him as he watches, or ask him to write the name and date independently.

Explain to the student that the following passage is from the beginning of a book called *Tom Sawyer,* by Mark Twain. Tom Sawyer is a little boy who lives with his Aunt Polly. He wants to go and play—but Aunt Polly has told him to go and whitewash (paint) the fence in front of the house first. Jim lives in the house and helps with the chores.

> Saturday morning was come, and all the summer world was bright and fresh, and brimming with life. There was a song in every heart; and if the heart was young the music issued at the lips. There was cheer in every face and a spring in every step. The locust-trees were in bloom and the fragrance of the blossoms filled the air. Cardiff Hill, beyond the village and above it, was green with vegetation and it lay just far enough away to seem a Delectable Land, dreamy, reposeful, and inviting.
>
> Tom appeared on the sidewalk with a bucket of whitewash and a long-handled brush. He surveyed the fence, and all gladness left him and a deep melancholy settled down upon his spirit. Thirty yards of board fence nine feet high. Life to him seemed hollow, and existence but a burden. Sighing, he dipped his brush and passed it along the topmost plank; repeated the operation; did it again; compared the insignificant whitewashed streak with the far-reaching continent of unwhitewashed fence, and sat down on a

> tree-box discouraged. Jim came skipping out at the gate with a tin pail, and singing Buffalo Gals. Bringing water from the town pump had always been hateful work in Tom's eyes, before, but now it did not strike him so. He remembered that there was company at the pump. … And he remembered that although the pump was only a hundred and fifty yards off, Jim never got back with a bucket of water under an hour—and even then somebody generally had to go after him. Tom said:
> "Say, Jim, I'll fetch the water if you'll whitewash some."

> —From *Tom Sawyer*
> by Mark Twain

Ask the following questions. Remind the student to answer you in complete sentences. If he answers in a fragment, turn the fragment into a complete sentence, say it to him, and then ask him to repeat this sentence back to you. If he cannot answer a question, read him the part of the passage that contains the answer, and then ask the question again.

Instructor: In the story, what day of the week is it?
Student: *It is Saturday.*

Instructor: What kind of trees were blooming?
Student: *Locust trees were blooming.*

Instructor: Can you remember the name of the hill beyond the village?
Student: *The hill was called Cardiff Hill.*

Instructor: Why was Tom Sawyer filled with melancholy?
Student: *He had to whitewash the fence.*

Instructor: What chore was Jim getting ready to do?
Student: *He was getting ready to bring water from the town pump.*

Instructor: Did Tom usually enjoy this chore?
Student: *No, he did not.*

Instructor: What did he suggest to Jim?
Student: *He said that he would get the water if Jim would whitewash.*

Ask, "What is one thing you remember about the passage?" Write the student's answer down on Student Page 82 as he watches. This answer can be the same as one of the answers above.

DAY THREE: Copywork   *Student Page 83*

Focus: *Beginning capitals and ending periods; capitalizing first (proper) names, and days of the week*

Pull out Student Page 83. Write the student's name and the date for him as he watches, or ask him to write the name and date independently.

The following model sentences are already printed on it:

Jim came skipping out at the gate with a tin pail.
Saturday morning was come, and all the summer world was bright and fresh, and brimming with life.

Ask the student to look carefully at the sentences. While he is examining the sentences, point out that "Jim" is capitalized because it is the proper name of a person, and "Saturday" is capitalized because it is the proper name of a day of the week. Even if these two words were not at the beginning of the sentences, they would still be capitalized. Ask the student what punctuation mark comes at the end of both sentences. Have him point to the two periods.

Choose whichever sentence is appropriate to the student's handwriting ability. Watch the student as he writes in pencil. If he begins to make an error, gently stop him and ask him to look at the model again.

DAY FOUR: Narration Exercise and Copywork   *Student Page 84*

Pull out Student Page 84. Write the student's name and the date for him as he watches, or ask him to write the name and date independently.

Read the following passage out loud to the student. Explain that Tom Sawyer can't convince Jim to do the whitewashing for him. Then Ben Rogers—a boy just about Tom's age—comes along the sidewalk. He starts to tease Tom, but then Tom has an idea about how to convince Ben to whitewash the fence for him.

Try to use different voices for Tom and for Ben Rogers (the first speech is spoken by Ben).

"Say—I'm going in a-swimming, I am. Don't you wish you could? But of course you'd druther *work*—wouldn't you? Course you would!"

Tom contemplated the boy a bit, and said:

"What do you call work?"

"Why, ain't *that* work?"

Tom resumed his whitewashing, and answered carelessly:

"Well, maybe it is, and maybe it ain't. All I know, is, it suits Tom Sawyer."

"Oh come, now, you don't mean to let on that you *like* it?"

The brush continued to move. "Like it? Well, I don't see why I oughtn't to like it. Does a boy get a chance to whitewash a fence every day?"

That put the thing in a new light. Ben stopped nibbling his apple. Tom swept his brush daintily back and forth—stepped back to note the effect—added a touch here and there—criticised the effect again—Ben watching every move and getting more and more interested, more and more absorbed. Presently he said:

"Say, Tom, let *me* whitewash a little."

Tom considered, was about to consent; but he altered his mind:

"No—no—I reckon it wouldn't hardly do, Ben. You see, Aunt Polly's awful particular about this fence—right here on the street, you know—but if it was the back fence I wouldn't mind and *she* wouldn't. Yes, she's awful particular about this fence; it's got to be done very careful; I reckon there ain't one boy in a thousand, maybe two thousand, that can do it the way it's got to be done."

"No—is that so? Oh come, now—lemme just try. Only just a little—I'd let *you*, if you was me, Tom."

—From *Tom Sawyer*
by Mark Twain

Ask the following questions. Remind the student to answer you in complete sentences. If he answers in a fragment, turn the fragment into a complete sentence, say it to him, and then ask him to repeat this sentence back to you. If he cannot answer a question, read him the part of the passage that contains the answer, and then ask the question again.

Instructor: What is Ben Rogers getting ready to do when he sees Tom?
Student: *He is going swimming.*

Instructor: Did Tom tell Ben that he liked painting the fence, or that he hated it?
Student: *He said that he liked painting the fence.*

Instructor: Do you think that he really *did* like painting the fence?
Student: *No, he was pretending.*

Instructor: After Ben watches Tom paint for a little while, what does he ask to do?
Student: *He asks to paint a little.*

Instructor: Does Tom let him?
Student: *No, Tom will not let him paint.*

Instructor: When Tom tells Ben that only one boy in two thousand can paint the fence properly, what does Ben want to do?
Student: *He wants to paint the fence too.*

Ask, "What is one thing you remember about the passage?" Write the student's answer down on the "Instructor" lines of Student Page 84 as he watches. This answer can be the same as one of the answers above.

Now ask the student to copy the sentence in pencil on the "Student" lines below the model. If the sentence is too long for comfort, he can copy only the first eight to ten words.

WEEK 22

DAY ONE: Copywork   *Student Page 85*

Focus: *Names of seasons*

Pull out Student Page 85. Write the student's name and the date for her as she watches, or ask her to write the name and date independently.

The following two model sentences are already printed on it:

> They played in the garden in spring.
> In spring, the boy and the rabbit spent long days in the garden.

Ask the student to look carefully at the sentences. While she is examining the sentences, explain that these sentences are about *The Velveteen Rabbit,* by Margery Williams Bianco. In the story, a toy rabbit wants to become a real rabbit. He has heard from other toys in the nursery that this can happen if the boy—his owner—really loves him.

Explain to the student that when we write the names of the seasons—summer, winter, fall, and spring—we do not begin the name of the season with a capital letter. In the sentences above, have the student point to the word "spring" in both sentences.

Choose whichever sentence is appropriate to the student's handwriting ability. Watch the student as she writes in pencil. If she begins to make an error, gently stop her and ask her to look at the model again.

DAY TWO: Narration Exercise   *Student Page 86*

Pull out Student Page 86. Write the student's name and the date for her as she watches, or ask her to write the name and date independently.

Tell the student that the following passage is from *The Velveteen Rabbit,* by Margery Williams Bianco. If the student asks why Boy and Rabbit are capitalized, tell her that in this story the boy's proper name is Boy and the rabbit's proper name is Rabbit.

> There was once a velveteen rabbit, and in the beginning he was really splendid. He was fat and bunchy, as a rabbit should be; his coat was spotted brown and white, he had real thread whiskers, and his ears were lined with pink sateen. On Christmas morning, when he sat wedged in the top of the Boy's stocking, with a sprig of holly between his paws, the effect was charming.
>
> There were other things in the stocking, nuts and oranges and a toy engine, and chocolate almonds and a clockwork mouse, but the Rabbit was quite the best of all. For at least two hours the Boy loved him, and then Aunts and Uncles came to dinner, and there was a great rustling of tissue paper and unwrapping of parcels, and in the excitement of looking at all the new presents, the Velveteen Rabbit was forgotten.

For a long time he lived in the toy cupboard or on the nursery floor, and no one thought very much about him. He was naturally shy, and being only made of velveteen, some of the more expensive toys quite snubbed him. The mechanical toys were very superior, and looked down upon every one else; they were full of modern ideas, and pretended they were real. The model boat, who had lived through two seasons and lost most of his paint, caught the tone from them and never missed an opportunity of referring to his rigging in technical terms. The Rabbit could not claim to be a model of anything, for he didn't know that real rabbits existed; he thought they were all stuffed with sawdust like himself, and he understood that sawdust was quite out-of-date and should never be mentioned in modern circles.

—From *The Velveteen Rabbit*
by Margery Williams Bianco

Ask the following questions. Remind the student to answer you in complete sentences. If she answers in a fragment, turn the fragment into a complete sentence, say it to her, and then ask her to repeat this sentence back to you. If she cannot answer a question, read her the part of the passage that contains the answer, and then ask the question again.

Instructor: What was the color of the rabbit's fur?
Student: *His coat was brown and white.*

Instructor: Can you remember the color of the rabbit's ears?
Student: *They were pink.*

Instructor: The story begins on a special holiday. Can you remember which one?
Student: *The story begins on Christmas Day.*

Instructor: The boy sees the rabbit on Christmas morning. Where is the rabbit when the boy finds him?
Student: *The rabbit is in the stocking.*

Instructor: There were other things in the boy's stocking. Can you remember two of them?
Student: *There were nuts and oranges, a toy engine, chocolate almonds, and a clockwork mouse.*

Instructor: Can you remember what thing in the stocking the boy loved best of all?
Student: *He loved the rabbit best of all.*

Instructor: Can you remember one other toy that was in the nursery with the rabbit?
Student: *There was a model boat.*

Ask, "What is one thing you remember about the passage?" Write the student's answer down on Student Page 86 as she watches. This answer can be the same as one of the answers above.

DAY THREE: Copywork   *Student Page 87*

Focus: Names of seasons

Pull out Student Page 87. Write the student's name and the date for her as she watches, or ask her to write the name and date independently.

The following model sentences are already printed on it:

> That was a wonderful summer.
> In the spring, the boy went out to play in the wood.

Ask the student to look carefully at the sentences. While she is examining the sentences, explain to the student that these sentences are taken from *The Velveteen Rabbit*. The first sentence tells about the summer during which the boy and rabbit played together nearly every day.

Ask the student to point to the names of the seasons in both sentences. Remind her that the names of seasons are not capitalized.

Choose whichever sentence is appropriate to the student's handwriting ability. Watch the student as she writes in pencil. If she begins to make an error, gently stop her and ask her to look at the model again.

DAY FOUR: Narration Exercise and Copywork   *Student Page 88*

Pull out Student Page 88. Write the student's name and the date for her as she watches, or ask her to write the name and date independently.

Read the following passage from *The Velveteen Rabbit* out loud to the student. In the passage the rabbit sees two real rabbits come up to look at him. He doesn't know that they are "real"—he thinks they are mechanical rabbits, like the wind-up toys in the nursery.

> Near the house where they lived there was a wood, and in the long June evenings the Boy liked to go there after tea to play. He took the Velveteen Rabbit with him, and before he wandered off to pick flowers, or play at brigands among the trees, he always made the Rabbit a little nest somewhere among the bracken, where he would be quite cozy, for he was a kind-hearted little boy and he liked Bunny to be comfortable.
>
> One evening, while the Rabbit was lying there alone, watching the ants that ran to and fro between his velvet paws in the grass, he saw two strange beings creep out of the tall bracken near him. They were rabbits like himself, but quite furry and brand-new. They must have been very well made, for their seams didn't show at all, and they changed shape in a queer way when they moved; one minute they were long and thin and the next minute fat and bunchy, instead of always staying the same like he did. Their feet padded softly on the ground, and they crept quite close to him, twitching their noses, while the Rabbit stared hard to see which side the clockwork stuck out, for

he knew that people who jump generally have something to wind them up. But he couldn't see it. They were evidently a new kind of rabbit altogether. They stared at him, and the little Rabbit stared back. And all the time their noses twitched.

"Why don't you get up and play with us?" one of them asked.

"I don't feel like it," said the Rabbit, for he didn't want to explain that he had no clockwork.

"Ho!" said the furry rabbit. "It's as easy as anything." And he gave a big hop sideways and stood on his hind legs.

—From *The Velveteen Rabbit*
by Margery Williams Bianco

Ask the following questions. Remind the student to answer you in complete sentences. If she answers in a fragment, turn the fragment into a complete sentence, say it to her, and then ask her to repeat this sentence back to you. If she cannot answer a question, read her the part of the passage that contains the answer, and then ask the question again.

Instructor: Where did the boy like to play during the long summer evenings?
Student: *He liked to play in the wood.*

Instructor: When the boy went to play in the wood, whom did he take with him?
Student: *He took the Velveteen Rabbit.*

Instructor: What did the boy make for the Velveteen Rabbit before he wandered off to play?
Student: *He made him a little nest.*

Instructor: What insects were running between the Velveteen Rabbit's paws?
Student: *The rabbit watched ants run between his paws.*

Instructor: What two animals did the rabbit see creep out of the wood?
Student: *He saw two rabbits.*

Instructor: The Velveteen Rabbit noticed several things about the rabbits that came up to look at him. Can you remember one of them?
Student: *He noticed that their seams didn't show; they could change their shape (when they hopped); and their noses twitched.*

Instructor: What did the two rabbits ask the Velveteen Rabbit to do?
Student: *They asked him to come and play with them.*

Ask, "What is one thing you remember about the passage?" Write the student's answer down on the "Instructor" lines of Student Page 88 as she watches. This answer can be the same as one of the answers above.

Now ask the student to copy the sentence in pencil on the "Student" lines below the model. If the sentence is too long for comfort, she can copy only the first eight to ten words.

WEEK 23

DAY ONE: Copywork   *Student Page 89*

Focus: *Review capitalizing first (proper) names, beginning capitals and ending periods*

Pull out Student Page 89. Write the student's name and the date for him as he watches, or ask him to write the name and date independently.

The following two model sentences are already printed on it:

> Billy dangled a leaf in front of the cat.
> Joe came scuffing up the walk and flopped down beside Billy.

Ask the student to look carefully at the sentences. While he is examining the sentences, explain that these sentences are from the book *How to Eat Fried Worms,* which tells the story of four friends who make a bet about whether or not they can eat worms. You will read a selection from the book in the next lesson.

Remind the student that first names are capitalized. Have him point to the names in both of the sentences. The first word of both sentences is capitalized not only because it is the first word in the sentence, but also because it is a first name. In the second sentence, "Billy" is capitalized because it is a first, or proper, name. Both sentences end with a period. Have the student use his or her pencil to point to the periods that end the sentences.

Choose whichever sentence is appropriate to the student's handwriting ability. Watch the student as he writes in pencil. If he begins to make an error, gently stop him and ask him to look at the model again.

DAY TWO: Narration Exercise   *Student Page 90*

Pull out Student Page 90. Write the student's name and the date for him as he watches, or ask him to write the name and date independently.

Tell the student that the following passage is from the first chapter of *How to Eat Fried Worms,* by Thomas Rockwell. Three friends—Tom, Alan, and Billy—are waiting for their friend Joe to come and play, and they are talking about why Tom's mother had kept him from playing with the rest of them last night. Tom explains that he had refused to eat even one bite of the salmon casserole his mother made for dinner. Billy tells Tom that he would eat one bite of *anything* to avoid being sent to his room. Most of the opening conversation is between Alan and Billy. You may want to use different voices as you read the selection.

> "How about worms?" Alan asked Billy.
> Tom's sister's cat squirmed out from under the porch and rubbed against Billy's knee.
> "Sure," said Billy. "Why not? Worms are just dirt."
> "Yeah, but they bleed."
> "So you'd have to cook them. Cows bleed."

"I bet a hundred dollars you wouldn't really eat a worm. You talk big now, but you wouldn't if you were sitting at the dinner table with a worm on your plate."

"I bet I would. I'd eat *fifteen* worms if somebody'd bet me a hundred dollars."

"You really want to bet? *I'll* bet you fifty dollars you can't eat fifteen worms. I really will."

"Where're you going to get fifty dollars?"

"In my savings account. I've got one hundred and thirty dollars and seventy-nine cents in my savings account. I know, because last week I put in the five dollars my grandmother gave me for my birthday."

"Your mother wouldn't let you take it out."

"She would if I lost the bet. She'd have to. I'd tell her I was going to sell my stamp collection otherwise. And I bought that with all my own money that I earned mowing lawns, so I can do whatever I want with it. I'll bet you fifty dollars you can't eat fifteen worms. Come on. You're chicken. You know you can't do it."

"*I* wouldn't do it," said Tom. "If salmon casserole makes me sick, think what fifteen worms would do."

Joe came scuffing up the walk and flopped down beside Billy. He was a small boy, with dark hair and a long nose and brown eyes.

"What's going on?"

"Come on," said Alan to Billy. "Tom can be your second and Joe'll be mine, just like in a duel. You think it's so easy—here's your chance to make fifty bucks."

Billy dangled a leaf in front of the cat, but the cat just rubbed against his knee, purring.

"What kind of worms?"

"Regular worms."

"Not those big green ones that get on the tomatoes. I won't eat those. And I won't eat them all at once. It might make me sick. One worm a day for fifteen days."

—From *How to Eat Fried Worms*
by Thomas Rockwell

Ask the following questions. Remind the student to answer you in complete sentences. If he answers in a fragment, turn the fragment into a complete sentence, say it to him, and then ask him to repeat this sentence back to you. If he cannot answer a question, read him the part of the passage that contains the answer, and then ask the question again.

Instructor: When Alan asks Billy if he would eat a worm, what does Billy say?
Student: *Billy says that yes, he would eat a worm.*

Instructor: Alan tells Billy that he would give Billy fifty dollars if Billy would eat fifteen worms. Where would he get the money for the bet?
Student: *Alan says that he would get the money from his savings account.*

Instructor: Billy says that Alan's mother might not let him take the money out of his savings account. If that happens, what would Alan sell to get the fifty dollars?
Student: *He says that he would sell his stamp collection.*

Instructor: Billy thinks about taking the bet. What kinds of worms does Alan say that Billy would have to eat?
Student: *He says he'd have to eat regular worms.*

Instructor: What kind of worm was Billy afraid of having to eat?
Student: *He didn't want to have to eat a green, tomato worm.*

Ask, "What is one thing you remember about the passage?" Write the student's answer down on Student Page 90 as he watches. This answer can be the same as one of the answers above.

DAY THREE: Copywork   *Student Page 91*

Focus: *Review capitalizing "I" in the middle of a sentence*

Pull out Student Page 91. Write the student's name and the date for him as he watches, or ask him to write the name and date independently.

The following model sentences are already printed on it:

> And I will not eat them all at once.
> Last week I put in the five dollars my grandmother gave me.

Ask the student to look carefully at the sentences. While he is examining the sentences, explain to the student that these sentences are also from *How to Eat Fried Worms,* by Thomas Rockwell.

Remind the student that "I" is a pronoun because it stands for a name—your name! Whenever you use the pronoun "I," it is always capitalized. Have the student point to the "I" in the two sentences.

Choose whichever sentence is appropriate to the student's handwriting ability. Watch the student as he writes in pencil. If he begins to make an error, gently stop him and ask him to look at the model again.

DAY FOUR: Narration Exercise and Copywork   *Student Page 92*

Pull out Student Page 92. Write the student's name and the date for him as he watches, or ask him to write the name and date independently.

Read the following passage from *How to Eat Fried Worms* out loud to the student. Explain that Billy *did* accept the bet to eat fifteen worms for fifty dollars from Alan. Now Alan, Tom, and Joe are preparing the first worm, while Billy is preparing himself to eat the worm. Explain to the student that when the passage says that Joe was acting "obsequiously," he was acting like a servant to Alan. Also, explain to the child that a night crawler is a larger-than-average earthworm, and can be up to eight inches long. Piccalilli is very much like relish or a salsa—often made from tomatoes, cucumbers, peppers, onions, vinegar, and sugar. And finally, you may want to use a bad French accent for Alan when he comes to present the worm—or as he says, the "Vurm"!

> He hadn't been able to think of anything special to do to prepare himself for eating a worm, so he was just limbering up in general—push-ups, knee bends, jumping jacks—red-faced, perspiring.
>
> Nearby, on an orange crate, he'd set out bottles of ketchup and Worchestershire sauce, jars of piccalilli and mustard, a box of crackers, salt and pepper shakers, a lemon, a slice of cheese, his mother's tin cinnamon-and-sugar shaker, a box of Kleenex, a jar of maraschino cherries, some horseradish, and a plastic honey bear.
>
> Tom's head appeared around the door.
>
> "Ready?"
>
> Billy scrambled up, brushing back his hair.
>
> "Yeah."
>
> "TA RAHHHHHHHHH!"
>
> Tom flung the door open; Alan marched in carrying a covered silver platter in both hands, Joe slouching along beside him with a napkin over one arm, nodding and smiling obsequiously. Tom dragged another orange crate over beside the first; Alan set the silver platter on it.
>
> "A chair," cried Alan. "A chair for the monshure!"
>
> "Come on," said Billy. "Cut the clowning."
>
> Tom found an old milking stool in one of the horse stalls. Joe dusted it off with his napkin, showing his teeth, and then ushered Billy onto it.
>
> "Luddies and gintlemin!" shouted Alan. "I prezint my musterpiece: Vurm a la Mud!"
>
> He swept the cover off the platter.
>
> "Awrgh!" cried Billy recoiling.
>
> The huge night crawler sprawled limply in the center of the plate, brown and steaming.
>
> "Boiled," said Tom. "We boiled it."
>
> Billy stormed about the barn, kicking barrels and posts, arguing. "A night crawler isn't a *worm!* If it was a worm, it'd be called a worm. A night crawler's a night crawler."

—From *How to Eat Fried Worms*
by Thomas Rockwell

Ask the following questions. Remind the student to answer you in complete sentences. If he answers in a fragment, turn the fragment into a complete sentence, say it to him, and then ask him to repeat this sentence back to you. If he cannot answer a question, read him the part of the passage that contains the answer, and then ask the question again.

> **Instructor:** What was one thing that Billy did as he prepared to eat the worm?
> **Student:** *He did push-ups, knee bends, and jumping jacks.*

> **Instructor:** Billy brought several different foods along to make his eating of the worm easier. Can you remember two of the foods he brought?
> **Student:** *He brought ketchup and Worchestershire sauce, jars of piccalilli and mustard, a box of crackers, salt and pepper shakers, a lemon, a slice of cheese, his mother's tin cinnamon-and-sugar shaker, a jar of maraschino cherries, some horseradish, and a plastic honey bear.*

> **Instructor:** Alan brought in the worm. On what had he placed the worm?
> **Student:** *He had placed it on a covered silver platter.*

> **Instructor:** Joe walked in behind Alan. What was he bringing in on his arm?
> **Student:** *He carried in a white napkin.*

> **Instructor:** What were the orange crates used for?
> **Student:** *The orange crates were used as the table. The boys put the silver platter on the orange crates.*

> **Instructor:** The boys had talked about cooking the worms different ways—fried, steamed, boiled. How was this one prepared?
> **Student:** *The boys had boiled this one.*

> **Instructor:** What kind of worm was it?
> **Student:** *It was a night crawler!*

> **Instructor:** What did Billy do when he saw the worm on the platter?
> **Student:** *He stomped around the barn and argued that this was not a worm.*

Ask, "What is one thing you remember about the passage?" Write the student's answer down on the "Instructor" lines of Student Page 92 as he watches. This answer can be the same as one of the answers above.

Now ask the student to copy the sentence in pencil on the "Student" lines below the model. If the sentence is too long for comfort, he can copy only the first eight to ten words.

WEEK 24

DAY ONE: Copywork   *Student Page 93*

Focus: *Abbreviating months of the year*

Pull out Student Page 93. Write the student's name and the date for her as she watches, or ask her to write the name and date independently.

The following names of the months are already printed on it:

January	_____
February	_____
March	_____
April	_____
May	(we do not abbreviate May)
June	_____
July	_____
August	_____
September	_____
October	_____
November	_____
December	_____

As the student watches, explain that we abbreviate months of the year by writing the first three letters of the month, followed by a period. Ask the student to point to the first three letters of January. Then, as she watches, write them on the line and place a period after them. Then do the same for February. Ask the student to say the first three letters of March. Remind her that she will write these three letters and follow them with a period to abbreviate March.

Have the student watch as you abbreviate the rest of the months on the list. If she begins to make an error, gently stop her and ask her to look at the model again. When you get to May, explain that we do not abbreviate May because it has only three letters.

Now ask the student to copy as many of the abbreviations as appropriate.

DAY TWO: Narration Exercise   *Student Page 94*

Pull out Student Page 94. Write the student's name and the date for her as she watches, or ask her to write the name and date independently. Instead of writing the student's full name, you may use initials for the student's first and middle names.

Tell the student that the following passage is from *The Happy Hollisters,* by Jerry West. The five Hollister children and their parents have just moved to a new house. The children love to solve mysteries, and as they move to the new house, they will find several that they must solve. In this lesson and in the next narration lesson, you will read about two of those mysteries. Pete and Pam, the eldest children, have decided to look around the outside of the house. If the child asks, tell her that a false face is a mask.

> Meanwhile, Pete and Pam had circled the house, and now stood looking at it. Suddenly Pam gasped and pointed to an attic window.
>
> "Pete, do you see what I see?"
>
> In the dusk she had seen what appeared to be a face. The next moment it disappeared.
>
> "It looked like a man," Pam quavered.

"But how could it be?" Pete argued.

"I guess it couldn't be," Pam agreed. "It might be a dummy or a false face somebody left up there."

"I'll find out," Pete offered.

"I'm going with you," Pam said, and dashed into the house after him and up the stairs.

Pete opened the door to the attic and clicked the light button. But the light did not go on.

"It's sure dark up there," he said. "I'd better get a flashlight."

He hurried to his bedroom and took his flashlight from his dresser. Returning to the dark stairway, he focused its beam upward.

"I'll go first," he told Pam.

Pete tiptoed slowly up the stairs, with his sister directly behind him. When they reached a landing, they stopped to listen. There was not a sound.

Pete went up a few more steps until his head was level with the attic floor. He beamed the light around.

"Maybe somebody was up here," Pam said in a whisper.

The children went up the remaining steps and stood listening.

"It's so spooky up here," Pam said, brushing a cobweb.

"I wonder why the light didn't go on," Pete said.

He directed his flash around to find the fixture. "Oh, I see. There's no bulb in it."

"I'll get one," Pam offered, glad to leave the attic for a minute.

She hurried down to the second floor and took a bulb from a socket in the hall, then returned and screwed it into the fixture. The attic was flooded with light.

"Now we can really explore," Pete said.

He opened a closet that had not been noticed before. The door to it squeaked and groaned. The closet was empty.

Next the boy walked over to the window, where Pam had thought she had seen the face.

"Wow!" Pete exclaimed. "Look at this!" and pointed to the sill. There were finger marks in the dust.

"Somebody was here," Pam said, "but where did he go?"

—From *The Happy Hollisters*
by Jerry West

Ask the following questions. Remind the student to answer you in complete sentences. If she answers in a fragment, turn the fragment into a complete sentence, say it to her, and then ask her to repeat this sentence back to you. If she cannot answer a question, read her the part of the passage that contains the answer, and then ask the question again.

Instructor: When Pete and Pam explore the outside of the house, what does Pam see?
Student: *Pam sees a face in an attic window.*

Instructor: Pete argues that it might not be a man's face. If it were not really a face, what does Pam say that it could be?
Student: *She says it could be a dummy or a false face.*

Instructor: When Pete and Pam go up to the attic and Pete flips the light switch, what happens?
Student: *The light does not turn on.*

Instructor: What does Pete get from his bedroom?
Student: *He runs to get a flashlight.*

Instructor: Pete uses the flashlight to find out why the light doesn't turn on. What does he find?
Student: *He sees that there is no lightbulb in the socket.*

Instructor: After Pam gets the lightbulb, what do she and Pete find?
Student: *They find and open the door to an empty closet.*

Instructor: At the end of their exploration, what does Pete see in the dust on the sill?
Student: *He sees finger marks OR fingerprints.*

Ask, "What is one thing you remember about the passage?" Write the student's answer down on Student Page 94 as she watches. This answer can be the same as one of the answers above.

DAY THREE: Copywork   *Student Page 95*

Focus: *Abbreviating months of the year*

Pull out Student Page 95. Write the student's name and the date for her as she watches, or ask her to write the name and date independently.

The following model sentences are already printed on it:

Today is _____, _____ _____, _____.
     (day of the week)   (month) (day) (year)

Today is _____, _____ _____, _____.
     (day of the week) (month abbrev.) (day) (year)

I was born on _____ _____, _____.
        (month) (day) (year)

I was born on _____ _____, _____.
    (month abbrev.) (day) (year)

As the student watches, write the appropriate day of the week, month, day of the month, and year in each blank in the first and third sentences. Remind the student that we abbreviate the month of the year by writing the first three letters of the month and by following it with a period. Fill in the blanks in the second and forth sentences, but this time, use the correct abbreviations for the months. (Note: if you are completing this exercise in May, or if the student's birthday is in May, you will have to explain that you cannot abbreviate May because it has only three letters.)

Choose whichever sentence—one that includes the abbreviation for the month—that is appropriate to the student's handwriting ability. Watch the student as she writes in pencil. If she begins to make an error, gently stop her and ask her to look at the model again.

DAY FOUR: Narration Exercise and Copywork   *Student Page 96*

Pull out Student Page 96. Write the student's name and the date for her as she watches, or ask her to write the name and date independently.

Read the following passage from *The Happy Hollisters,* by Jerry West. On one of the first few mornings at their new house, while other family members are exploring the house itself, Holly and Pam decide to take their rowboat out on the lake nearby for a short expedition. Neither of the girls is experienced with the rowboat.

Pam untied the rope which held the boat to the dock, and then shoved off. Holly was not very skillful at rowing and splashed the oars up and down. Pam had to keep dodging so the water from them would not soak her. Before they knew it, the girls were in deeper water.

"Oh, see that big black cloud!" cried Holly, looking up.

"It's going to rain," shouted Pam. "We'd better get back to shore."

Holly had often seen Pete whirl the boat around fast by holding one oar in the water and rowing hard with the other. She would try this.

But as she did so, both oars slipped from her hands. They jerked clear out of the oarlocks and landed in the water. Before Pam could grab them, they had drifted away from the boat.

"Oh dear," wailed Holly, "what'll we do?"

Pam knew she must not become panicky. "We'll paddle with our hands," she decided in desperation.

The two girls started to paddle this way as fast as they could. But by this time a strong wind had begun to blow, moving the boat farther and farther from shore. The girls cried for help, but their voices were lost in the strong gale. Soon they were in the middle of the lake, with whitecaps slapping at the side of the boat. Then the shore of Blackberry Island came into sight. The wind was blowing them right toward it! When the rowboat touched the shore, Pam hopped out and helped Holly up on the pebbly beach.

"Oh, I'm glad we're here," said Holly with a sigh of relief. "But how'll we get home?"

"Just wait for somebody to come and rescue us," Pam answered hopefully.

After a slight sprinkle of rain, the storm cloud passed over, and the wind died down. Pam took Holly's hand, and they walked along the shore together.

"Do you suppose anybody lives here?" Holly asked her sister.

"Daddy said there used to be a farmhouse on this island once," Pam replied, "but nobody lives in it now."

"Somebody's been here today," Holly said. "Look!"

She pointed to a group of loose stones in the sand. It was a crude fireplace with a few blackened embers. There was still warmth in them.

—From *The Happy Hollisters*
by Jerry West

Ask the following questions. Remind the student to answer you in complete sentences. If she answers in a fragment, turn the fragment into a complete sentence, say it to her, and then ask her to repeat this sentence back to you. If she cannot answer a question, read her the part of the passage that contains the answer, and then ask the question again.

Instructor: The girls got in the boat and drifted into deeper water. What did Holly see in the sky?
Student: *She saw a storm cloud.*

Instructor: What happened when Holly tried to turn the boat in the same way her brother, Pete, did?
Student: *The oars slipped and fell into the water.*

Instructor: How did the girls paddle once they'd lost their oars?
Student: *They used their hands as oars.*

Instructor: The girls drifted into an island. Can you remember the name of the island?
Student: *The girls drifted to Blackberry Island.*

Instructor: The storm passed over, and the girls walked along the shore of the island. What did Holly ask her sister?
Student: *She asked her if she thought anyone lived on the island.*

Instructor: What evidence did the girls see that led them to believe that someone had been on the island recently?
Student: *The girls saw a crude fireplace that still had some warm embers.*

Ask, "What is one thing you remember about the passage?" Write the student's answer down on the "Instructor" lines of Student Page 96 as she watches. This answer can be the same as one of the answers above.

Now ask the student to copy the sentence in pencil on the "Student" lines below the model. If the sentence is too long for comfort, she can copy only the first eight to ten words.

WEEK 25

DAY ONE: Copywork   *Student Page 97*

Focus: *Proper usage of "sit" and "set"*

Pull out Student Page 97. Write the student's name and the date for him as he watches, or ask him to write the name and date independently.

The following two model sentences are already printed on it:

> Now sit down, please, right here.
> She used to come and sit on our doorstep with the kids.

Ask the student to look carefully at the sentences. While he is examining the sentences, explain that these sentences are adapted from the book *Pollyanna*, which tells the story of a young girl who comes to live with her aunt. Ask the student to point to the word "sit" in each of the sentences. Explain that we use "sit" if we mean "to sit down" or "to rest." We use "set" if we are referring to putting or placing an object.

Choose whichever sentence is appropriate to the student's handwriting ability. Watch the student as he writes in pencil. If he begins to make an error, gently stop him and ask him to look at the model again.

DAY TWO: Narration Exercise   *Student Page 98*

Pull out Student Page 98. Write the student's name and the date for him as he watches, or ask him to write the name and date independently.

Tell the student that the following passage is from *Pollyanna*, by Eleanor Porter. Nancy is a young woman who has taken a job doing housework for the wealthy Miss Polly Harrington, who lives alone. Miss Polly has just received news of her sister's death, and is preparing for her niece, Pollyanna, to come and live with her.

> Nancy stifled a sigh. She was wondering if ever in any way she could please this woman. Nancy had never "worked out" before; but a sick mother suddenly widowed and left with three younger children besides Nancy herself, had forced the girl into doing something toward their support, and she had been so pleased when she found a place in the kitchen of the great house on the hill—Nancy had come from "The Corners," six miles away, and she knew Miss Polly Harrington only as the mistress of the old Harrington homestead, and one of the wealthiest residents of the town. That was two months before. She knew Miss Polly now as a stern, severe-faced woman who

frowned if a knife clattered to the floor, or if a door banged—but who never thought to smile even when knives and doors were still.

"When you've finished your morning work, Nancy," Miss Polly was saying now, "you may clear the little room at the head of the stairs in the attic, and make up the cot bed. Sweep the room and clean it, of course, after you clear out the trunks and boxes."

"Yes, ma'am. And where shall I put the things, please, that I take out?"

"In the front attic." Miss Polly hesitated, then went on: "I suppose I may as well tell you now, Nancy. My niece, Miss Pollyanna Whittier, is coming to live with me. She is eleven years old, and will sleep in that room."

"A little girl—coming here, Miss Harrington? Oh, won't that be nice!" cried Nancy, thinking of the sunshine her own little sisters made in the home at "The Corners."

"Nice? Well, that isn't exactly the word I should use," rejoined Miss Polly, stiffly. "However, I intend to make the best of it, of course. I am a good woman, I hope; and I know my duty."

—From *Pollyanna*
by Eleanor Porter

Ask the following questions. Remind the student to answer you in complete sentences. If he answers in a fragment, turn the fragment into a complete sentence, say it to him, and then ask him to repeat this sentence back to you. If he cannot answer a question, read him the part of the passage that contains the answer, and then ask the question again.

Instructor: What is the name of the person now working in Miss Polly Harrington's house?
Student: *Her name is Nancy.*

Instructor: What is Miss Polly like, according to Nancy?
Student: *Miss Polly is a stern, severe woman.*

Instructor: According to Nancy, does Miss Polly smile a lot?
Student: *No, she does not!*

Instructor: What job does Miss Polly ask Nancy to do when she finishes her morning work?
Student: *She asks her to clean the room at the head of the stairs in the attic and to make up the bed.*

Instructor: Miss Polly tells Nancy why she is doing this cleaning. Can you remember the reason?
Student: *Miss Polly says that her niece is coming to live with her.*

Instructor: Nancy is excited to hear that 11-year-old Pollyanna is coming to live with them. Can you remember Miss Polly's reaction?
Student: *She says that she is doing her duty, and that she plans to make the best of it.*

Ask, "What is one thing you remember about the passage?" Write the student's answer down on Student Page 98 as he watches. This answer can be the same as one of the answers above.

DAY THREE: Copywork   *Student Page 99*

Focus: *Proper usage of "sit" and "set"*

Pull out Student Page 99. Write the student's name and the date for him as he watches, or ask him to write the name and date independently.

The following model sentences are already printed on it:

> She set the pitcher down at once.
> Pollyanna was disappointed, and she set the bowl of jelly down.

Ask the student to look carefully at the sentences. While he is examining the sentences, explain that these sentences are from the book *Pollyanna*, by Eleanor Porter. Ask the student to point to the word "set" in each of the sentences. Then ask him what object is being set down in each of the two sentences. Remind the student that we use "sit" if we mean "to sit down" or "to rest." We use "set" if we are referring to putting or placing an object.

Choose whichever sentence is appropriate to the student's handwriting ability. Watch the student as he writes in pencil. If he begins to make an error, gently stop him and ask him to look at the model again.

DAY FOUR: Narration Exercise and Copywork   *Student Page 100*

Pull out Student Page 100. Write the student's name and the date for him as he watches, or ask him to write the name and date independently.

Read the following passage from *Pollyanna*. The day has come to pick up Pollyanna from the train station, and Miss Polly sends Nancy and Timothy to meet Pollyanna and bring her to the house. Timothy is another worker at Miss Polly's, and he is friends with Nancy. Pollyanna is expecting to see her aunt, Miss Polly, at the train station and so when she sees Nancy, she mistakes her for her aunt.

> Promptly at twenty minutes to four the next afternoon Timothy and Nancy drove off in the open buggy to meet the expected guest. Timothy was Old Tom's son. It was sometimes said in the town that if Old Tom was Miss Polly's right-hand man, Timothy was her left.
>
> Timothy was a good-natured youth, and a good-looking one, as well. Short as had been Nancy's stay at the house, the two were already good friends. To-day, however, Nancy was too full of her mission to be her usual talkative self; and almost in silence she took the drive to the station and alighted to wait for the train.

Over and over in her mind she was saying, "Light hair, red-checked dress, straw hat." Over and over again she was wondering just what sort of child this Pollyanna was, anyway.

"I hope for her sake she's quiet and sensible, and don't drop knives nor bang doors," she sighed to Timothy, who had sauntered up to her.

"Well, if she ain't, nobody knows what'll become of the rest of us," grinned Timothy. "Imagine Miss Polly and a NOISY kid! Gorry! there goes the whistle now!"

"Oh, Timothy, I—I think it was mean ter send me," chattered the suddenly frightened Nancy, as she turned and hurried to a point where she could best watch the passengers alight at the little station.

It was not long before Nancy saw her—the slender little girl in the red-checked gingham with two fat braids of flaxen hair hanging down her back. Beneath the straw hat, an eager, freckled little face turned to the right and to the left, plainly searching for some one.

Nancy knew the child at once, but not for some time could she control her shaking knees sufficiently to go to her. The little girl was standing quite by herself when Nancy finally did approach her.

"Are you Miss—Pollyanna?" she faltered. The next moment she found herself half smothered in the clasp of two gingham-clad arms.

"Oh, I'm so glad, GLAD, GLAD to see you," cried an eager voice in her ear. "Of course I'm Pollyanna, and I'm so glad you came to meet me! I hoped you would."

"You—you did?" stammered Nancy, vaguely wondering how Pollyanna could possibly have known her—and wanted her. "You—you did?" she repeated, trying to straighten her hat.

"Oh, yes; and I've been wondering all the way here what you looked like," cried the little girl, dancing on her toes, and sweeping the embarrassed Nancy from head to foot, with her eyes.

"And now I know, and I'm glad you look just like you do look."

—From *Pollyanna*
by Eleanor Porter

Ask the following questions. Remind the student to answer you in complete sentences. If he answers in a fragment, turn the fragment into a complete sentence, say it to him, and then ask him to repeat this sentence back to you. If he cannot answer a question, read him the part of the passage that contains the answer, and then ask the question again.

Instructor: What was the name of the boy who went with Nancy to pick up Pollyanna at the train station?
Student: *His name was Timothy.*

Instructor: Nancy was usually talkative with her friend Timothy. Did she and Timothy talk a lot on the way to the train station?
Student: *No—she was not her usual, talkative self.*

Instructor: Nancy knew a few things about what Pollyanna looked like, and she repeated these details to herself so she would be able to find her at the station. Can you remember two of those details?
Student: *Nancy knew that Pollyanna had light hair, a red-checked dress, and a straw hat.*

Instructor: What did Nancy hope that Pollyanna would be like?
Student: *Nancy hoped that Pollyanna was quiet and sensible.*

Instructor: What did Pollyanna do when Nancy came up to her?
Student: *Pollyanna put her arms around Nancy and gave her a hug.*

Instructor: Pollyanna said she was glad that Nancy had come. What had Pollyanna been wondering about during her trip?
Student: *She tells Nancy she'd been wondering what she looked like the entire trip.*

Ask, "What is one thing you remember about the passage?" Write the student's answer down on the "Instructor" lines of Student Page 100 as he watches. This answer can be the same as one of the answers above.

Now ask the student to copy the sentence in pencil on the "Student" lines below the model. If the sentence is too long for comfort, he can copy only the first eight to ten words.

WEEK 26

Day One: Copywork   *Student Page 101*

Focus: *Abbreviating titles of respect*

Pull out Student Page 101. Write the student's name and the date for her as she watches, or ask her to write the name and date independently.

The following two model sentences are already printed on it:

> From here they looked down into the garden of Mr. McGregor.
> The gig was driven by Mr. McGregor, and beside him sat Mrs. McGregor in her best bonnet.

Ask the student to look carefully at the sentences. While she is examining the sentences, explain that these sentences are adapted from *The Tale of Benjamin Bunny*, by Beatrix Potter. In the story, Peter Rabbit and his cousin Benjamin Bunny go on an adventure into Mr. McGregor's garden.

Explain to the student that when titles of respect are written, they are often abbreviated. When she abbreviates titles of respect, tell her that:

Mr. stands for Mister.

Dr. stands for Doctor.

Mrs. refers to a married woman.

Miss refers to an unmarried woman. (Miss is not abbreviated.)

Ms. can refer to any woman.

Have the student point to the titles of respect in the sentences above.

Choose whichever sentence is appropriate to the student's handwriting ability. Watch the student as she writes in pencil. If she begins to make an error, gently stop her and ask her to look at the model again.

DAY TWO: Narration Exercise   *Student Page 102*

Pull out Student Page 102. Write the student's name and the date for her as she watches, or ask her to write the name and date independently.

Tell the student that the following passage is from *The Tale of Benjamin Bunny*, by Beatrix Potter. If the student asks what "relations" are, explain that that is another word for relatives—in this case, Benjamin is going to see his cousins.

> One morning a little rabbit sat on a bank.
> He pricked his ears and listened to the trit-trot, trit-trot of a pony.
> A gig was coming along the road; it was driven by Mr. McGregor, and beside him sat Mrs. McGregor in her best bonnet.
> As soon as they had passed, little Benjamin Bunny slid down into the road, and set off—with a hop, skip and a jump—to call upon his relations, who lived in the wood at the back of Mr. McGregor's garden.
> That wood was full of rabbit holes; and in the neatest sandiest hole of all, lived Benjamin's aunt and his cousins—Flopsy, Mopsy, Cottontail and Peter.
> Old Mrs. Rabbit was a widow; she earned her living by knitting rabbit-wool mittens and muffetees (I once bought a pair at a bazaar). She also sold herbs, and rosemary tea, and rabbit-tobacco (which is what *we* call lavender).
>
> —From *The Tale of Benjamin Bunny*
> by Beatrix Potter

Ask the following questions. Remind the student to answer you in complete sentences. If she answers in a fragment, turn the fragment into a complete sentence, say it to her, and then ask her to repeat this sentence back to you. If she cannot answer a question, read her the part of the passage that contains the answer, and then ask the question again.

Instructor: What did the rabbit hear coming along the road?
Student: *He heard the trit-trot of a pony.*

Instructor: Who was driving the gig?
Student: *Mr. McGregor was driving it.*

Instructor: Who was sitting next to Mr. McGregor, and what was she wearing?
Student: *Mrs. McGregor was sitting next to him, and she was wearing a bonnet.*

Instructor: As soon as the horse and gig had passed, who slid down into the road to go see his relatives?
Student: *Benjamin Bunny went to go see his relatives, at the back of Mr. McGregor's garden.*

Instructor: Four rabbits, who were living in the neatest and sandiest hole, were named in the story. Can you remember two of their names?
Student: *The rabbits' names are Flopsy, Mopsy, Cottontail, and Peter.*

Instructor: We find out what Mrs. Rabbit does to earn a living. Can you remember one of the items that she knits, and one of the items that she sells?
Student: *She knits mittens and muffetees, and she sells herbs, rosemary tea, and rabbit-tobacco.*

Ask, "What is one thing you remember about the passage?" Write the student's answer down on Student Page 102 as she watches. This answer can be the same as one of the answers above.

DAY THREE: Copywork   *Student Page 103*

Focus: *Abbreviating titles of respect*

Pull out Student Page 103. Write the student's name and the date for her as she watches, or ask her to write the name and date independently.

The following model sentences are already printed on it:

> Old Mrs. Rabbit was a widow.
> The name of the father of Benjamin was Mr. Benjamin Bunny.

Ask the student to look carefully at the sentences. While she is examining the sentences, explain to the student that these sentences are adapted from *The Tale of Benjamin Bunny*. Then ask the student which titles of respect she is able to remember from the copywork lesson earlier this week. (If this is too difficult, ask her what "Mr." stands for, and move down the list by asking the same question of each of the abbreviations for the titles of respect.) After she has listed all that she can remember, go over the list below:

Mr. stands for Mister.

Dr. stands for Doctor.

Mrs. refers to a married woman.

Miss refers to an unmarried woman. (Miss is not abbreviated.)

Ms. can refer to any woman.

Finally, have the student point to the titles of respect in the sentences above.

Choose whichever sentence is appropriate to the student's handwriting ability. Watch the student as she writes in pencil. If she begins to make an error, gently stop her and ask her to look at the model again.

DAY FOUR: Narration Exercise and Copywork   *Student Page 104*

Pull out Student Page 104. Write the student's name and the date for her as she watches, or ask her to write the name and date independently.

Read the following passage from *The Tale of Benjamin Bunny* out loud to the student. In a previous book with the same characters, Peter Rabbit had been nearly caught by Mr. McGregor. On trying to escape from Mr. McGregor, Peter lost his coat and shoes. Benjamin and Peter go to the garden to retrieve Peter's clothes, now hanging on the scarecrow in the middle of the garden. If the student asks what a tam-o'-shanter is, explain that it is a round, wool hat with a pom-pom in the center.

> Little Benjamin said, "It spoils people's clothes to squeeze under a gate; the proper way to get in, is to climb down a pear tree."
>
> Peter fell down head first; but it was of no consequence, as the bed below was newly raked and quite soft.
>
> It had been sown with lettuces.
>
> They left a great many odd little foot-marks all over the bed, especially little Benjamin, who was wearing clogs.
>
> Little Benjamin said that the first thing to be done was to get back Peter's clothes, in order that they might be able to use the pocket handkerchief.
>
> They took them off the scarecrow. There had been rain during the night; there was water in the shoes, and the coat was somewhat shrunk.
>
> Benjamin tried on the tam-o'-shanter, but it was too big for him.
>
> Then he suggested that they should fill the pocket-handkerchief with onions, as a little present for his Aunt.
>
> —From *The Tale of Benjamin Bunny*
> by Beatrix Potter

Ask the following questions. Remind the student to answer you in complete sentences. If she answers in a fragment, turn the fragment into a complete sentence, say it to her, and then ask her to repeat this sentence back to you. If she cannot answer a question, read her the part of the passage that contains the answer, and then ask the question again.

Instructor: Why did Benjamin object to squeezing under the gate to get into the garden?
Student: *He said that climbing under a gate spoils people's clothes.*

Instructor: Instead of squeezing under a gate, how did Benjamin recommend getting into a garden?
Student: *He said the best way to get into the garden was to climb down a pear tree.*

Instructor: Peter ended up falling into the garden. Why wasn't he hurt?
Student: *The dirt below had been newly raked, and it was soft.*

Instructor: The rabbits were going to the garden to get something. Can you remember what it was?
Student: *They were going to get back Peter's clothes.*

Instructor: When they were in the garden, where did Peter and Benjamin find the clothes?
Student: *They found them on the scarecrow.*

Instructor: What did Peter and Benjamin decide to bring back as a present for Mrs. Rabbit?
Student: *They were going to bring her a present of onions.*

Ask, "What is one thing you remember about the passage?" Write the student's answer down on the "Instructor" lines of Student Page 104 as she watches. This answer can be the same as one of the answers above.

Now ask the student to copy the sentence in pencil on the "Student" lines below the model. If the sentence is too long for comfort, she can copy only the first eight to ten words.

WEEK 27

DAY ONE: Copywork

Student Page 105

Focus: *Abbreviating titles of respect*

Pull out Student Page 105. Write the student's name and the date for him as he watches, or ask him to write the name and date independently.

The following two model sentences are already printed on it:

> In came Mrs. Fezziwig, one vast substantial smile.
> I have the pleasure of addressing Mr. Scrooge and Mr. Marley.

Ask the student to look carefully at the sentences. While he is examining the sentences, explain that these sentences are adapted from *A Christmas Carol*, by Charles Dickens. In the book, a miserly old man, Mr. Ebenezer Scrooge, meets three spirits who help him to become a better man. You will read a selection from the book in the next lesson.

Explain to the student that when titles of respect are written, they are often abbreviated. When he abbreviates titles of respect, remind him that:

Mr. stands for Mister.

Dr. stands for Doctor.

Mrs. refers to a married woman.

Miss refers to an unmarried woman. (Miss is not abbreviated.)

Ms. can refer to any woman.

Have the student point to the titles of respect in the sentences above.

Choose whichever sentence is appropriate to the student's handwriting ability. Watch the student as he writes in pencil. If he begins to make an error, gently stop him and ask him to look at the model again.

DAY TWO: Narration Exercise   *Student Page 106*

Pull out Student Page 106. Write the student's name and the date for him as he watches, or ask him to write the name and date independently.

Tell the student that the following passage is from *A Christmas Carol*, by Charles Dickens. On a cold Christmas Eve in London, a bitter old man, Mr. Ebenezer Scrooge, works at his business with his clerk, or assistant, Bob Cratchit. His nephew, Fred, comes by the office to wish him a Merry Christmas.

> Once upon a time—of all the good days in the year, on Christmas Eve—old Scrooge sat busy in his counting-house. It was cold, bleak, biting weather: foggy withal: and he could hear the people in the court outside, go wheezing up and down, beating their hands upon their breasts, and stamping their feet upon the pavement stones to warm them. The city clocks had only just gone three, but it was quite dark already—it had not been light all day— and candles were flaring in the windows of the neighbouring offices, like ruddy smears upon the palpable brown air. The fog came pouring in at every chink and keyhole, and was so dense without, that although the court was of the narrowest, the houses opposite were mere phantoms. To see the dingy cloud come drooping down, obscuring everything, one might have thought that Nature lived hard by, and was brewing on a large scale.
>
> The door of Scrooge's counting-house was open that he might keep his eye upon his clerk, who in a dismal little cell beyond, a sort of tank, was copying letters. Scrooge had a very small fire, but the clerk's fire was so very much smaller that it looked like one coal. But he couldn't replenish it, for Scrooge kept the coal-box in his own room; and so surely as the clerk came in with the shovel, the master predicted that it would be necessary for them to part. Wherefore the clerk put on his white comforter, and tried to warm himself at the candle; in which effort, not being a man of a strong imagination, he failed.
>
> "A merry Christmas, uncle! God save you!" cried a cheerful voice. It was the voice of Scrooge's nephew, who came upon him so quickly that this was the first intimation he had of his approach.

"Bah!" said Scrooge, "Humbug!"

He had so heated himself with rapid walking in the fog and frost, this nephew of Scrooge's, that he was all in a glow; his face was ruddy and handsome; his eyes sparkled, and his breath smoked again.

"Christmas a humbug, uncle!" said Scrooge's nephew. "You don't mean that, I am sure?"

"I do," said Scrooge. "Merry Christmas! What right have you to be merry? What reason have you to be merry? You're poor enough."

"Come, then," returned the nephew gaily. "What right have you to be dismal? What reason have you to be morose? You're rich enough."

Scrooge having no better answer ready on the spur of the moment, said, "Bah!" again; and followed it up with "Humbug."

—From *A Christmas Carol*
by Charles Dickens

Ask the following questions. Remind the student to answer you in complete sentences. If he answers in a fragment, turn the fragment into a complete sentence, say it to him, and then ask him to repeat this sentence back to you. If he cannot answer a question, read him the part of the passage that contains the answer, and then ask the question again.

Instructor: The story begins on a holiday. Can you remember which one?
Student: The story begins on Christmas Eve.

Instructor: Where is Mr. Scrooge at the beginning of the passage?
Student: Mr. Scrooge is in his counting-house OR his office.

Instructor: We get many descriptions of the weather. Can you remember what it was like outside on this Christmas Eve?
Student: It was foggy, cold, cloudy, and dark outside.

Instructor: Scrooge kept the door of his office open so that he could keep his eye on someone. Can you remember who it was?
Student: He was keeping his eye on his clerk OR helper.

Instructor: How large was the clerk's fire, in comparison to Scrooge's?
Student: The clerk's fire was much smaller than Scrooge's.

Instructor: Who came to say hello to Mr. Scrooge?
Student: Scrooge's nephew came to wish him a Merry Christmas.

Instructor: What was Mr. Scrooge's response?
Student: Scrooge said, "Bah! Humbug!" and continued in his bad mood.

Ask, "What is one thing you remember about the passage?" Write the student's answer down on Student Page 106 as he watches. This answer can be the same as one of the answers above.

DAY THREE: Copywork

Focus: Abbreviating titles of respect

Pull out Student Page 107. Write the student's name and the date for him as he watches, or ask him to write the name and date independently.

The following model sentences are already printed on it:

> Mr. Scrooge it was.
> In came the three Miss Fezziwigs, beaming and lovable.

Ask the student to look carefully at the sentences. While he is examining the sentences, explain to the student that these sentences are from *A Christmas Carol.* Then ask the student which titles of respect he is able to remember from the copywork lesson earlier this week. (If this is too difficult, ask him what "Mr." stands for, and move down the list by asking the same question of each of the abbreviations for the titles of respect.) After he has listed all that he can remember, go over the list below:

Mr. stands for Mister.

Dr. stands for Doctor.

Mrs. refers to a married woman.

Miss refers to an unmarried woman. (Miss is not abbreviated.)

Ms. can refer to any woman.

Finally, have the student point to the titles of respect in the sentences above.

Choose whichever sentence is appropriate to the student's handwriting ability. Watch the student as he writes in pencil. If he begins to make an error, gently stop him and ask him to look at the model again.

DAY FOUR: Narration Exercise and Copywork

Pull out Student Page 108. Write the student's name and the date for him as he watches, or ask him to write the name and date independently.

Read the following passage from *A Christmas Carol* out loud to the student. In the book, three ghosts take Scrooge on three separate journeys during the night before Christmas. The first calls himself the Ghost of Christmas Past. He takes Scrooge back to watch a scene in which Scrooge, as a young man, is working for his first employer with his friend Dick Wilkins. Both Scrooge and Dick are apprentices, which means that both are learning the job from their employer. This employer, whom Scrooge admired and loved, is named Fezziwig. The work day comes to an end and the mood is merry, in contrast with Scrooge's mood earlier in the day when his nephew came to wish him Merry Christmas.

It was made plain enough, by the dressing of the shops, that here too it was Christmas time again; but it was evening, and the streets were lighted up.

The Ghost stopped at a certain warehouse door, and asked Scrooge if he knew it.

"Know it!" said Scrooge. "Was I apprenticed here!"

They went in. At sight of an old gentleman in a Welsh wig, sitting behind such a high desk, that if he had been two inches taller he must have knocked his head against the ceiling, Scrooge cried in great excitement:

"Why, it's old Fezziwig! Bless his heart; it's Fezziwig alive again!"

Old Fezziwig laid down his pen, and looked up at the clock, which pointed to the hour of seven. He rubbed his hands; adjusted his capacious waistcoat; laughed all over himself, from his shoes to his organ of benevolence; and called out in a comfortable, oily, rich, fat, jovial voice:

"Yo ho, there! Ebenezer! Dick!"

Scrooge's former self, now grown a young man, came briskly in, accompanied by his fellow-'prentice.

"Dick Wilkins, to be sure!" said Scrooge to the Ghost. "Bless me, yes. There he is. He was very much attached to me, was Dick. Poor Dick! Dear, dear!"

"Yo ho, my boys!" said Fezziwig. "No more work to-night. Christmas Eve, Dick. Christmas, Ebenezer! Let's have the shutters up," cried old Fezziwig, with a sharp clap of his hands, "before a man can say Jack Robinson!"

You wouldn't believe how those two fellows went at it! They charged into the street with the shutters—one, two, three—had 'em up in their places—four, five, six—barred 'em and pinned 'em—seven, eight, nine—and came back before you could have got to twelve, panting like race-horses.

"Hilli-ho!" cried old Fezziwig, skipping down from the high desk, with wonderful agility. "Clear away, my lads, and let's have lots of room here! Hilli-ho, Dick! Chirrup, Ebenezer!"

Clear away! There was nothing they wouldn't have cleared away, or couldn't have cleared away, with old Fezziwig looking on. It was done in a minute. Every movable was packed off, as if it were dismissed from public life for evermore; the floor was swept and watered, the lamps were trimmed, fuel was heaped upon the fire; and the warehouse was as snug, and warm, and dry, and bright a ball-room, as you would desire to see upon a winter's night.

In came a fiddler with a music-book, and went up to the lofty desk, and made an orchestra of it, and tuned like fifty stomach-aches. In came Mrs. Fezziwig, one vast substantial smile. In came the three Miss Fezziwigs, beaming and lovable. In came the six young followers whose hearts they broke. In came all the young men and women employed in the business. In came the housemaid, with her cousin, the baker. In came the cook, with her brother's particular friend, the milkman. In came the boy from over the way, who was suspected of not having board enough from his master; trying to hide himself behind the girl from next door but one, who was proved to have had her ears pulled by her mistress. In they all came, one after another; some shyly, some boldly, some gracefully, some awkwardly, some pushing, some pulling; in they all came, anyhow and everyhow.

—From *A Christmas Carol*
by Charles Dickens

Ask the following questions. Remind the student to answer you in complete sentences. If he answers in a fragment, turn the fragment into a complete sentence, say it to him, and then ask him to repeat this sentence back to you. If he cannot answer a question, read him the part of the passage that contains the answer, and then ask the question again.

Instructor: Scrooge and the Ghost stop at a door. Can you remember where they stopped?
Student: *They stopped at the place where Scrooge was apprenticed OR where he first learned his job.*

Instructor: Scrooge saw his old boss sitting at a tall desk. What was his name?
Student: *His name was Fezziwig.*

Instructor: What was the name of the other apprentice who worked with Scrooge and for Fezziwig?
Student: *His name was Dick Wilkins.*

Instructor: At seven o' clock, Fezziwig asked his workers to do something. Can you remember what job they had to do?
Student: *They had to put the shutters up.*

Instructor: Did they do the job slowly or quickly?
Student: *They did it quickly.*

Instructor: After the shutters were up, young Ebenezer and Dick had other jobs to do. Can you remember one of those jobs?
Student: *They moved the furniture off of the floor and then swept it; they tended the lamps and the fire.*

Instructor: After the room was ready, a musician came in to play for the Christmas party. Can you remember what instrument he played?
Student: *He played the fiddle OR He was a fiddler.*

Instructor: Many people came in to the party. Can you remember who two of them were?
Student: *Mrs. Fezziwig came, along with her three daughters. Six young men came following the daughters. The housemaid and her cousin, the cook, the milkman, and the boy from over the way.*

Ask, "What is one thing you remember about the passage?" Write the student's answer down on the "Instructor" lines of Student Page 108 as he watches. This answer can be the same as one of the answers above.

Now ask the student to copy the sentence in pencil on the "Student" lines below the model. If the sentence is too long for comfort, he can copy only the first eight to ten words.

WEEK 28

DAY ONE: Copywork   *Student Page 109*

Focus: *Capitalizing first names; abbreviating titles of respect*

Pull out Student Page 109. Ask the student to write her name and the date on the correct lines. From this point onwards, she should be able to do this herself.

The following two model sentences are already printed on it:

> In the morning Mr. Scott slid down the rope and dug.
> The buckets came up full of mud, and Pa and Mr. Scott worked every day in deeper mud.

Explain to the student that these sentences are from *Little House on the Prairie,* another book written by Laura Ingalls Wilder. After the events in *Little House in the Big Woods,* which we read from back in Week 1, the Ingalls family moved away from their little Wisconsin house, further west into unsettled land. There were no other houses or towns on the prairies (huge, wide open fields) where they decided to settle down, so Laura's father and another settler, Mr. Scott, had to dig a well so that the family could have clean drinking water.

Choose whichever sentence is appropriate to the student's handwriting ability. Watch the student as she writes in pencil. If she begins to make an error, gently stop her and ask her to look at the model again.

DAY TWO: Narration Exercise   *Student Page 110*

Pull out Student Page 110. Ask the student to write her name and the date on the correct lines.

Explain to the student that today's narration describes the end of the well-digging project. For days, Pa and Mr. Scott have been taking turns going down into the hole, digging up the dirt at the bottom, and sending it back up to the surface in a bucket. They have to dig until the hole is deep enough to reach "ground water"—the water that collects in pools under the earth's surface.

You may need to explain that "bailing" is taking out bucketfuls of water and dumping them somewhere else.

> There began to be a little water in the well, but it was not enough. The buckets came up full of mud, and Pa and Mr. Scott worked every day in deeper mud. In the mornings when the candle went down, it lighted oozing-wet walls, and candlelight sparkled in rings over the water when the bucket struck bottom.
>
> Pa stood knee deep in water and bailed out bucketfuls before he could begin digging in the mud.

One day when he was digging, a loud shout came echoing up. Ma ran out of the house and Laura ran to the well. "Pull, Scott! Pull!" Pa yelled. A swishing, gurgling sound echoed down there. Mr. Scott turned the windlass as fast as he could, and Pa came up climbing hand over hand up the rope.

"I'm blamed if that's not quicksand!" Pa gasped, as he stepped onto the ground, muddy and dripping. "I was pushing down hard on the spade, when all of a sudden it went down, the whole length of the handle. And water came pouring up all around me."

—From *Little House on the Prairie*
by Laura Ingalls Wilder

Ask the following questions. Remind the student to answer you in complete sentences. If she answers in a fragment, turn the fragment into a complete sentence, say it to her, and then ask her to repeat this sentence back to you. If she cannot answer a question, read her the part of the passage that contains the answer, and then ask the question again.

Instructor: What did Pa and Mr. Scott use for light while they were digging in the hole?
Student: They had to use a candle.

Instructor: What did Pa have to do before he could start digging?
Student: He had to bail out water.

Instructor: How did Pa get up out of the well?
Student: He climbed up the rope.

Instructor: What did Pa find in the bottom of the well?
Student: There was quicksand in the bottom of the well.

Instructor: What happened when Pa pushed down hard on his spade?
Student: Water came pouring up.

Ask, "What is one thing you remember about the passage?" Write the student's answer down on Student Page 110 as she watches. This answer can be the same as one of the answers above.

DAY THREE: Copywork   *Student Page 111*

Pull out Student Page 111. Ask the student to write her name and the date on the correct lines. The following model sentences are already printed on it:

Grasshoppers beat down from the sky and swarmed thick over the ground.
Millions and millions of grasshoppers were eating now. You could hear the millions of jaws biting and chewing.

Explain that these sentences come from the next book about the Ingalls family, *On the Banks of Plum Creek.* Pa, Ma, Laura, and Laura's sisters have moved again. Now they are living in Minnesota, trying to make a living by farming. But their corn, barley, and garden vegetables are all eaten by swarms of grasshoppers who sweep down over their farm.

Ask the student to copy one, two, or three sentences, depending on handwriting ability. Watch the student as she writes in pencil. If she begins to make an error, gently stop her and ask her to look at the model again.

DAY FOUR: Narration Exercise and Copywork   *Student Page 112*

Pull out Student Page 112. Ask the student to write her name and the date on the correct lines.

Explain to the student that, when the grasshoppers first appeared, Laura didn't realize that she was looking at a swarm of insects. There were so many of them that she thought they were a stormcloud! (In the story, Jack is the family's dog.)

> A cloud was over the sun. It was not like any cloud they had ever seen before. It was a cloud of something like snowflakes, but they were larger than snowflakes, and thin and glittering. Light shone through each flickering particle.
>
> There was no wind. The grasses were still and the hot air did not stir, but the edge of the cloud came on across the sky faster than wind. The hair stood up on Jack's neck. All at once he made a frightful sound up at that cloud, a growl and a whine.
>
> Plunk! something hit Laura's head and fell to the ground. She looked down and saw the largest grasshopper she had ever seen. Then huge brown grasshoppers were hitting the ground all around her, hitting her head and her face and her arms. They came thudding down like hail.
>
> The cloud was hailing grasshoppers. The cloud *was* grasshoppers. Their bodies hid the sun and made darkness. Their thin, large wings gleamed and glittered. The rasping whirring of their wings filled the whole air and they hit the ground and the house with the noise of a hailstorm.
>
> Laura tried to beat them off. Their claws clung to her skin and her dress. They looked at her with bulging eyes, turning their heads this way and that. Mary ran screaming into the house. Grasshoppers covered the ground, there was not one bare bit to step on. Laura had to step on grasshoppers and they smashed squirming and slimy under her feet.

—From *On the Banks of Plum Creek*
by Laura Ingalls Wilder

Ask the following questions. Remind the student to answer you in complete sentences. If she answers in a fragment, turn the fragment into a complete sentence, say it to her, and then ask her to repeat this sentence back to you. If she cannot answer a question, read her the part of the passage that contains the answer, and then ask the question again.

Instructor: What did Laura think that the grasshopper cloud looked like?
Student: *It looked like a cloud of snowflakes.*

Instructor: Was the wind blowing?
Student: *No, there was no wind.*

Instructor: What did Jack the dog do when he saw the cloud?
Student: *He growled and hair stood up on his neck.*

Instructor: What did the grasshopper cloud do to the sun?
Student: *It hid the sun.*

Instructor: What kind of eyes did the grasshoppers have?
Student: *They had bulging eyes.*

Instructor: What did Mary do?
Student: *She ran into the house screaming.*

Instructor: What happened when Laura stepped on the ground?
Student: *She stepped on grasshoppers and they smashed under her feet.*

Ask, "What is one thing you remember about the passage?" Write the student's answer down on the "Instructor" lines of Student Page 112 as she watches. This answer can be the same as one of the answers above.

Now ask the student to copy the sentence in pencil on the "Student" lines below the model. She should attempt to complete the entire sentence.

WEEK 29

DAY ONE: Copywork   *Student Page 113*

***Focus:** Capitalizing first names; abbreviating titles of respect*

Pull out Student Page 113. Ask the student to write his name and the date on the correct lines. The following two model sentences are already printed on it:

> I am Miss Allen, your new librarian.
> You know how Tillie never takes a book out herself, but she is always wanting to read mine.

Explain to the student that these sentences are adapted from *All-of-a-Kind Family*, by Sydney Taylor, which tells the story of five young sisters who grow up in the city of New York about one hundred years ago. You will read a passage from the book in the next lesson.

Have the student point to the title of respect in the first sentence (he should point to "Miss"). Then have him point to the first, and proper, name in the second sentence. Remind him that first names always begin with a capital letter.

Choose whichever sentence is appropriate to the student's handwriting ability. Watch the student as he writes in pencil. If he begins to make an error, gently stop him and ask him to look at the model again.

Day Two: Narration Exercise   *Student Page 114*

Pull out Student Page 114. Ask the student to write his name and the date on the correct lines.

All-of-a-Kind Family is about a family living in New York in the early 1900s. In the following passage, four sisters—Ella, Henny, Charlotte, and Gertie—are waiting for their fifth sister, Sarah, to return from school. As soon as Sarah arrives, they all plan to go to the library for their weekly trip. Sarah finally comes home, but she is late—and she's in tears.

> Mama came over and sat down beside Sarah. Gently she stroked her hair and let the child weep. After a while she said softly, "Sarah, tell us what happened."
>
> Between sobs, the muffled words came slowly, "My—library book—is—lost."
>
> Lost! The children looked at each other in dismay. Such a thing had never happened in the family before. "Ooh—how awful!" Ella said, and then was sorry that the words had escaped her for they seemed to bring on a fresh burst of tears.
>
> "Now, now, stop crying, Sarah," Mama said. "You'll only make yourself sick. Come, we'll wash your face and then you'll tell us all about it."
>
> Obediently Sarah followed Mama to the kitchen sink.
>
> "Does it mean we can't go to the library ever again?" Charlotte whispered to Ella.
>
> Ella shook her head. "I don't think so."
>
> "Maybe we could change over to another branch," suggested Henny.
>
> The cold water felt good on Sarah's flushed face. She was quiet now and could talk.
>
> "It wasn't really me that lost the book. It was my friend, Tillie. You know how Tillie never takes a book out herself, but she's always wanting to read mine. When I told her about *Peter and Polly in Winter*, she begged me to lend it to her. She promised she'd give it back to me on Friday.
>
> "When I asked for it today, she said that she put it in my desk yesterday, but Mama, she didn't! She really didn't!"
>
> "Are you sure?" asked Mama. "Maybe you left it in school."
>
> "I looked a thousand times. That's why I came so late. I kept hunting and hunting all over the schoolroom."

"Maybe you brought it home with you yesterday and left it here in the house."

"Then it should be on the shelf under the whatnot," Ella said.

Hopefully, everybody rushed over to the whatnot where the library books were kept, but alas, there was no Peter and Polly book there today.

"I cleaned the house pretty thoroughly this morning," said Mama. "I don't remember seeing the book anywhere. But let's look again anyway."

How anxiously everyone searched. The children peered into every corner of the two bedrooms and they poked under beds and dressers. No one believed it was in the front room, but still they searched it diligently. They searched and searched until they had to agree that it was useless to continue.

When they were back in the kitchen again, Sarah said tearfully, "How can I go and tell the library that the book is lost?" She was ready to cry again.

"I'm afraid they won't let you take out any more books until we pay for this one," Mama said. "And a book costs a lot of money."

—From *All-of-a-Kind Family*
by Sydney Taylor

Ask the following questions. Remind the student to answer you in complete sentences. If he answers in a fragment, turn the fragment into a complete sentence, say it to him, and then ask him to repeat this sentence back to you. If he cannot answer a question, read him the part of the passage that contains the answer, and then ask the question again.

Instructor: Sarah was sitting down and crying. Why was she crying?
Student: *She had lost her library book.*

Instructor: What did Sarah's mother do to help Sarah calm down?
Student: *She took her to the kitchen sink and washed her face.*

Instructor: Sarah explains that she didn't really lose her book. Who does she say really lost her book?
Student: *She says that Tillie, a girl from school, lost her book.*

Instructor: Can you remember the name of the lost library book?
Student: *The name of the book is* Peter and Polly in Winter.

Instructor: Sarah says that she has looked and looked, and that the book is definitely not at school. Mama says that she has cleaned the house thoroughly. But what do the children do anyway?
Student: *They search every corner of the house.*

Instructor: What did Mama say that Sarah would have to do before she could take out more library books?
Student: *She would have to pay for the library book.*

Ask, "What is one thing you remember about the passage?" Write the student's answer down on Student Page 114 as he watches. This answer can be the same as one of the answers above.

DAY THREE: Copywork   *Student Page 115*

Focus: *Review capitalizing first names*

Pull out Student Page 115. Ask the student to write his name and the date on the correct lines. The following model sentences are already printed on it:

> Sarah studied the new library lady anxiously.
> She has dimples, Sarah thought. Surely a lady with dimples could never be harsh.

Ask the student to look carefully at the sentences. While he is examining the sentences, explain that both are from *All-of-a-Kind Family*. Sarah and her sisters have gone to the library to explain that she has lost her library book, and to find out what will happen because of that.

Choose whichever sentences are appropriate to the student's handwriting ability. Watch the student as he writes in pencil. If he begins to make an error, gently stop him and ask him to look at the model again.

DAY FOUR: Narration Exercise and Copywork   *Student Page 116*

Pull out Student Page 116. Ask the student to write his name and the date on the correct lines.

Read the following passage out loud to the student. Explain that Sarah and her sisters go to the library to tell the library lady about the lost book. They wait for Sarah to get up to the front of the line.

> Sarah studied the new library lady anxiously. She looked so fresh and clean in a crisp white shirtwaist with long sleeves ending in paper cuffs pinned tightly at the wrists. Her hair is light, just like mine, Sarah said to herself. And she has such little ears. I think she has a kind face. She watched as the librarian's slender fingers pulled the cards in and out of the index file. How does she keep her nails so clean, Sarah wondered, thinking of her own scrubby ones.
>
> It was Ella's turn to have her book stamped. The library lady looked up and Sarah could see the deep blue of her eyes. The library lady smiled.
>
> She has dimples, Sarah thought. Surely a lady with dimples could never be harsh.
>
> The smile on the library lady's face deepened. In front of her desk stood five little girls dressed exactly alike.
>
> "My goodness! Are you all one family?"
>
> "Yes, all one family," Henny spoke up. "I'm Henrietta, Henny for short; I'm ten. Ella's twelve, Sarah is eight, Charlotte is six, and Gertie is four."

"A steps-and-stairs family!" The library lady laughed and the tiny freckles on her pert nose seemed to laugh with her.

"That's a good name for us," Ella said. "Some people call us an all-of-a-kind family."

"All of a very nice kind," smiled the library lady. "And you have such nice names! I'm Miss Allen, your new librarian. I'm very glad to meet you."

Her eyes traveled over the five little girls. Such sad-looking faces. Not a smile among them.

"Better tell the teacher what happened," Charlotte whispered to Sarah.

"She's not a teacher, silly. She's a library lady." Henny's scornful reply was loud enough for Miss Allen to hear. The dimples began to show again.

Sarah stepped forward. "Library lady," she began, twisting and untwisting the fingers of her hands.

Miss Allen looked at Sarah and suddenly noticed the red-rimmed eyes and the nose all swollen from weeping. Something was wrong. No wonder the faces were so unhappy.

"Let me see, now. Which one are you?" she asked.

"Sarah," the little girl replied and the tears began to swim in her eyes.

The library lady put her hand under the little girl's chin and lifted it up. "Now, now, Sarah. Nothing can be that bad."

Sarah said tearfully, "Yes, it can. I—I —" She couldn't go on.

"Here." Ella put a handkerchief to her sister's nose.

Miss Allen went on speaking as if she did not notice anything unusual. "Did you enjoy your book?"

Sarah's voice broke. "I loved it. But nobody else will ever be able to read it again..."

"She means she lost it!" Henny blurted out.

—From *All-of-a-Kind Family*
by Sydney Taylor

Ask the following questions. Remind the student to answer you in complete sentences. If he answers in a fragment, turn the fragment into a complete sentence, say it to him, and then ask him to repeat this sentence back to you. If he cannot answer a question, read him the part of the passage that contains the answer, and then ask the question again.

Instructor: Sarah looks closely at what the new library lady looks like. Can you remember two of the details that Sarah notices about the library lady's appearance?
Student: *Sarah notices that she has light hair, a kind face, little ears, slender fingers, clean finger nails, blue eyes, and dimples.*

Instructor: Sarah also notices what the library lady is wearing. Can you remember what color shirt she is wearing?
Student: *She's wearing a white shirt.*

Instructor: The library lady notices something about how the five sisters are dressed. What does she notice?
Student: *She notices that the girls are dressed exactly alike.*

Instructor: Can you remember two of the names of the sisters?
Student: *The sisters are named Ella, Henrietta (OR Henny), Charlotte, Gertie, and Sarah.*

Instructor: Can you remember the name of the librarian?
Student: *Her name is Miss Allen.*

Instructor: What question did Miss Allen ask Sarah about the book?
Student: *She asked her if Sarah had enjoyed the book.*

Instructor: Did Sarah enjoy her book?
Student: *Yes, she did.*

Instructor: Can you remember which sister told the library lady that Sarah had lost the book?
Student: *Henny told the library lady that Sarah had lost it.*

Ask, "What is one thing you remember about the passage?" Write the student's answer down on the "Instructor" lines of Student Page 116 as he watches. This answer can be the same as one of the answers above.

Now ask the student to copy the sentence in pencil on the "Student" lines below the model. He should attempt to complete the entire sentence.

WEEK 30

DAY ONE: Copywork   *Student Page 117*

Focus: *Review forming commas*

Pull out Student Page 117. Ask the student to write her name and the date on the correct lines. The following two model sentences are already printed on it:

Splash, splash, splash, went her tears again.
Once upon a time there was a deep and wide river, and in this river
    lived a crocodile.

Explain to the student that these sentences are from "The Crocodile and the Monkey," which she will read in the next lesson. In the story, a crocodile and his wife try to outwit a monkey who lives in the trees near their river. The story is from a collection of Buddhist stories known as the Jataka Tales.

Point out the commas in each of the sentences. Ask the student to practice making commas at the bottom of Student Page 117. Remind her that commas are like periods with little tails that curve off to the left.

Choose whichever sentence is appropriate to the student's handwriting ability. Watch the student as she writes in pencil. If she begins to make an error, gently stop her and ask her to look at the model again.

DAY TWO: Narration Exercise   *Student Page 118*

Pull out Student Page 118. Ask the student to write her name and the date on the correct lines.

Explain to the student that today's narration comes from a collection of Buddhist stories called the Jataka Tales.

Once upon a time there was a deep and wide river, and in this river lived a crocodile. I do not know whether you have ever seen a crocodile; but if you did see one, I am sure you would be frightened. They are very long, twice as long as your bed; and they are covered with hard green or yellow scales; and they have a wide flat snout, and a huge jaw with hundreds of sharp teeth, so big that it could hold you all at once inside it. This crocodile used to lie all day in the mud, half under water, basking in the sun, and never moving; but if any little animal came near, he would jump up, and open his big jaws, and snap it up as a dog snaps up a fly. And if you had gone near him, he would have snapped you up, too, just as easily.

On the bank of this river lived a monkey. He spent the day climbing about the trees, and eating nuts or wild fruit; but he had been there so long, that there was hardly any fruit left upon the trees.

Now it happened that the crocodile's wife cast a longing eye on this Monkey. She was very dainty in her eating, was Mrs. Crocodile, and she liked the tid-bits. So one morning she began to cry. Crocodile's tears are very big, and as her tears dropped into the water, splash, splash, splash, Mr. Crocodile woke up from his snooze, and looked round to see what was the matter.

"Why, wife," said he, "what are you crying about?"

"I'm hungry!" whimpered Mrs. Crocodile.

"All right," said he, "wait a while. I'll soon catch you something."

"But I want that Monkey's heart!" said Mrs. Crocodile. Splash, splash, splash, went her tears again.

"Come, come, cheer up," said Mr. Crocodile. He was very fond of his wife, and he would have wiped away her tears, only he had no pocket-handkerchief. "Cheer up!" said he; "I'll see what I can do."

—From *The Giant Crab and Other Tales from Old India*
retold by W. H. D. Rouse

Ask the following questions. Remind the student to answer you in complete sentences. If she answers in a fragment, turn the fragment into a complete sentence, say it to her, and then ask her to repeat this sentence back to you. If she cannot answer a question, read her the part of the passage that contains the answer, and then ask the question again.

Instructor: The crocodile is described in detail. Can you remember how long a crocodile is?
Student: *A crocodile is twice as long as a bed.*

Instructor: Can you remember one of the colors that a crocodile's scales may be?
Student: *His scales may be green or yellow.*

Instructor: Did the Crocodile like to move around a lot during the day, or did he like to sit around and bask in the sun?
Student: *He liked to sit around and bask in the sun.*

Instructor: A monkey lived in the trees on a bank of the river where the crocodile lived. He had lived there so long that he had a problem. Can you remember what it was?
Student: *There was hardly any fruit left on the trees.*

Instructor: A splash from the water woke up Mr. Crocodile. What was the splashing?
Student: *The splashing was from Mrs. Crocodile's tears.*

Instructor: Why was Mrs. Crocodile crying?
Student: *She was crying because she was hungry.*

Instructor: What did Mrs. Crocodile want to eat?
Student: *She wanted to eat the monkey's heart.*

Instructor: What did Mr. Crocodile say to his wife?
Student: *He said that he would see what he could do about catching the monkey.*

Ask, "What is one thing you remember about the passage?" Write the student's answer down on Student Page 118 as she watches. This answer can be the same as one of the answers above.

DAY THREE: Copywork   *Student Page 119*

Focus: *Review initials as abbreviations for proper names*

Pull out Student Page 119. Ask the student to write her name and the date on the correct lines. The following model sentences are already printed on it:

W. H. D. Rouse wrote new versions of many Jataka Tales.
W. H. D. Rouse, along with T. E. Page, edited a series of famous books about classic works of literature.

Ask the student to look carefully at the sentences. While she is examining the sentences, explain to the student that these sentences are about the author of "The Crocodile and the

Monkey." Ask the student to point to the initials in Mr. Rouse's name. Remind her that an initial is the first letter of a person's name, followed by a period. Initials are capital letters, because names begin with capital letters.

Choose whichever sentence is appropriate to the student's handwriting ability. Watch the student as she writes in pencil. If she begins to make an error, gently stop her and ask her to look at the model again.

DAY FOUR: Narration Exercise and Copywork   *Student Page 120*

Pull out Student Page 120. Ask the student to write her name and the date on the correct lines.

Explain to the student that Mr. Crocodile finally thinks of a plan to trap the monkey, so that he can capture him for his wife.

You may need to explain that a quince is a fruit that looks much like an apple or a pear, and is used to make jelly, jam, or pudding.

"Monkey, dear!" called the Crocodile again.

"Well, what is it?" asked the Monkey.

"I'm sure you must be hungry," said Mr. Crocodile. "I see you have eaten all the fruit on these trees; but why don't you try the trees on the other side of the river? Just look, apples, pears, quinces, plums, anything you could wish for! And heaps of them!"

"That is all very well," said the Monkey. "But how can I get across a wide river like this?"

"Oh!" said the cunning Crocodile, "that is easily managed. I like your looks, and I want to do you a good turn. Jump on my back, and I'll swim across; then you can enjoy yourself!"

Never had the Monkey had an offer so tempting. He swung round a branch three times in his joy; his eyes glistened, and without thinking a moment, down he jumped on the Crocodile's back.

The Crocodile began to swim slowly across. The Monkey fixed his eyes on the opposite bank with its glorious fruit trees, and danced for joy. Suddenly he felt the water about his feet! It rose to his legs, it rose to his middle. The Crocodile was sinking!

"Mr. Crocodile! Mr. Crocodile! Take care!" said he. "You'll drown me!"

"Ha, ha, ha!" laughed the Crocodile, snapping his great jaws. "So you thought I was taking you across out of pure good nature! You are a green monkey, to be sure. The truth is, my wife has taken a fancy to you, and wants your heart to eat! If you had seen her crying this morning, I am sure you would have pitied her."

"What a good thing you told me!" said the Monkey. (He was a very clever Monkey, and had his wits about him.) "Wait a bit, and I'll tell you why. My heart, I think you said? Why I never carry my heart inside me; that would be too dangerous. If we Monkeys went jumping about the trees with our hearts inside, we should knock them to bits in no time."

The Crocodile rose up to the surface again. He felt very glad he had not drowned the Monkey, because, as I said, he was a stupid creature, and did not see that the Monkey was playing him a trick.

"Oh," said he, "where is your heart, then?"

"Do you see that cluster of round things up in the tree there, on the further bank? Those are our hearts, all in a bunch; and pretty safe too, at that height, I should hope!" It was really a fig tree, and certainly the figs did look like a bunch of hearts. "Just you take me across," he went on, "and I'll climb up and drop my heart down; I can do very well without it."

"You excellent creature!" said the Crocodile, "so I will!"

—From *The Giant Crab and Other Tales from Old India*
retold by W. H. D. Rouse

Ask the following questions. Remind the student to answer you in complete sentences. If she answers in a fragment, turn the fragment into a complete sentence, say it to her, and then ask her to repeat this sentence back to you. If she cannot answer a question, read her the part of the passage that contains the answer, and then ask the question again.

Instructor: What did Mr. Crocodile tell the monkey was just on the other side of the river?
Student: He told him about the trees with apples, pears, quinces, and plums.

Instructor: The monkey was excited about the fruit trees, but he had a problem. What was it?
Student: He couldn't get to the other side of the river.

Instructor: What did Mr. Crocodile offer to do for him?
Student: Mr. Crocodile offered to take him across the river.

Instructor: Did the monkey accept Mr. Crocodile's offer to take him across?
Student: Yes, he did accept the offer.

Instructor: What did Mr. Crocodile begin to do on his swim across the river?
Student: He began to sink.

Instructor: When the monkey called out to Mr. Crocodile, what did Mr. Crocodile tell the monkey?
Student: He told the monkey that he was taking him back to his wife, who wanted to eat his heart.

Instructor: When he heard this bad news, what did the monkey tell Mr. Crocodile?
Student: He told Mr. Crocodile that it would be much too dangerous to keep his heart inside of him.

Instructor: When Mr. Crocodile asked where he kept his heart, what did the monkey say?
Student: He said it was up in the fig tree.

Instructor: Did Mr. Crocodile seem to believe the monkey?
Student: *Yes, he did.*

Ask, "What is one thing you remember about the passage?" Write the student's answer down on the "Instructor" lines of Student Page 120 as she watches. This answer can be the same as one of the answers above.

Now ask the student to copy the sentence in pencil on the "Student" lines below the model. She should attempt to complete the entire sentence.

WEEK 31

DAY ONE: Copywork   *Student Page 121*

Focus: *Capitalizing lines of poetry*

Pull out Student Page 121. Ask the student to write his name and the date on the correct lines. The following lines of poetry are already printed on it:

> Across the lonely beach we flit,
> One little sandpiper and I,
> And fast I gather, bit by bit,
> The scattered driftwood, bleached and dry.

Explain to the student that these lines of poetry are from "The Sandpiper," by Celia Thaxter. The poem is about a young girl who runs down the shore to collect driftwood before a storm. While she is running, she watches a sandpiper—a small shorebird—run along with her.

Explain to the student that the first word in every line of the poem begins with a capital letter.

Watch the student as he writes in pencil. If he begins to make an error, gently stop him and ask him to look at the model again. If the entire selection is too long for comfort, have the student copy only the first two lines.

DAY TWO: Narration Exercise   *Student Page 122*

Pull out Student Page 122. Ask the student to write his name and the date on the correct lines.

Explain to the student that you are going to read him a poem called "The Sandpiper," written by Celia Thaxter. The poem is about a girl who is running along the beach before a storm. The child sees a sandpiper—a small shorebird—and notices that the bird is running along the shore, too. Tell the student that he needs to listen carefully to what the girl in the poem is doing, to what she sees as she is running along the beach, and to what she thinks about the sandpiper.

Across the lonely beach we flit,
One little sandpiper and I,
And fast I gather, bit by bit,
The scattered driftwood, bleached and dry.
The wild waves reach their hands for it,
The wild wind raves, the tide runs high,
As up and down the beach we flit,
One little sandpiper and I.

Above our heads the sullen clouds
Scud, black and swift, across the sky;
Like silent ghosts in misty shrouds
Stand out the white lighthouses high.
Almost as far as eye can reach
I see the close-reefed vessels fly,
As fast we flit along the beach,
One little sandpiper and I.

I watch him as he skims along,
Uttering his sweet and mournful cry;
He starts not at my fitful song,
Nor flash of fluttering drapery.
He has no thought of any wrong,
He scans me with a fearless eye;
Staunch friends are we, well tried and strong,
The little sandpiper and I.

Comrade, where wilt thou be tonight,
When the loosed storm breaks furiously?
My driftwood fire will burn so bright!
To what warm shelter canst thou fly?
I do not fear for thee, though wroth
The tempest rushes through the sky:
For are we not God's children both,
Thou, little sandpiper, and I?

> —From "The Sandpiper"
> by Celia Thaxter

Ask the following questions. Remind the student to answer you in complete sentences. If he answers in a fragment, turn the fragment into a complete sentence, say it to him, and then ask him to repeat this sentence back to you. If he cannot answer a question, read him the part of the poem that contains the answer, and then ask the question again.

Instructor: What is the young girl gathering as she runs along the shore?
Student: *She is gathering driftwood.*

Instructor: Can you remember how many sandpipers are running along the shore with the girl?

Student: *The girl sees one sandpiper running along the shore.*

Instructor: The child describes the weather. Can you remember if it is windy outside?

Student: *Yes, it is windy outside.*

Instructor: The child also describes the color of the storm clouds. Can you remember what color they are?

Student: *The clouds are black.*

Instructor: The clouds are black, which stand out against the color of the lighthouses. Can you remember the color of the lighthouses?

Student: *The lighthouses are white.*

Instructor: The child calls the sandpiper her friend, or comrade. As she thinks about the coming storm, what does the child wonder about the sandpiper?

Student: *She wonders where he will find shelter.*

Instructor: In the end, the child says she does not fear for the sandpiper. Can you remember why?

Student: *She does not fear for the sandpiper because both the child and the sandpiper are cared for by God.*

Ask, "What is one thing you remember about the passage?" Write the student's answer down on Student Page 122 as he watches. This answer can be the same as one of the answers above.

DAY THREE: Copywork   *Student Page 123*

Focus: *Capitalizing lines of poetry*

Pull out Student Page 123. Ask the student to write his name and the date on the correct lines. The following lines of poetry are already printed on it:

> A nightingale, that all day long
> Had cheered the village with his song,
> Nor yet at eve his note suspended,
> Nor yet when eventide was ended,
> Began to feel, as well he might,
> The keen demands of appetite.

Explain to the student that these lines of poetry are from "The Nightingale and the Glow-worm," by William Cowper. The poem is about a nightingale who is tired and hungry at the end of a long day of singing for the village.

Remind the student that the first word in every line of the poem begins with a capital letter.

Choose the appropriate number of lines (2–6) for the student to copy. Watch the student as he writes in pencil. If he begins to make an error, gently stop him and ask him to look at the model again.

DAY FOUR: Narration Exercise and Copywork   *Student Page 124*

Pull out Student Page 124. Ask the student to write his name and the date on the correct lines.

Explain to the student that you are going to read him a poem called "The Nightingale and the Glow-worm," written by William Cowper. The poem is about a nightingale, a songbird, who is tired and hungry at the end of the day. Tell the student that he needs to listen carefully to what the nightingale is planning to do, and to what the glow-worm says to the nightingale in response.

You may need to explain to the student that a "hawthorn" is a tree; "crop" is another word for throat; "quoth" is another word for said; "minstrelsy" is singing; and "to abhor" means to hate.

> A nightingale, that all day long
> Had cheered the village with his song,
> Nor yet at eve his note suspended,
> Nor yet when eventide was ended,
> Began to feel, as well he might,
> The keen demands of appetite;
> When, looking eagerly around,
> He spied far off, upon the ground,
> A something shining in the dark,
> And knew the glow-worm by his spark;
> So, stooping down from hawthorn top,
> He thought to put him in his crop.
> The worm, aware of his intent,
> Harangued him thus, right eloquent.
> "Did you admire my lamp," quoth he,
> "As much as I your minstrelsy,
> You would abhor to do me wrong,
> As much as I to spoil your song;
> For 'twas the self-same power divine
> Taught you to sing and me to shine;
> That you with music, I with light,
> Might beautify and cheer the night."
> The songster heard his short oration,
> And warbling out his approbation,

> Released him, as my story tells,
> And found a supper somewhere else.

—From "The Nighingale and the Glow-worm"
by William Cowper

Ask the following questions. Remind the student to answer you in complete sentences. If he answers in a fragment, turn the fragment into a complete sentence, say it to him, and then ask him to repeat this sentence back to you. If he cannot answer a question, read him the part of the poem that contains the answer, and then ask the question again.

Instructor: What does the nightingale do for the village all day long?
Student: *He sings for the village OR He cheers the village with his song.*

Instructor: At the end of the day, what feeling does the nightingale have?
Student: *At the end of the day, the nightingale is hungry.*

Instructor: What does the nightingale see when he is looking around for food?
Student: *He sees a glow-worm.*

Instructor: Before the nightingale eats the worm, what does the worm ask him?
Student: *The worm asks if the nightingale admires his lamp.*

Instructor: The worm says that he admires the nightingale's minstrelsy, or singing. He says that both singing, and his lamp, are gifts. Who, does he say, has given these gifts?
Student: *He says that the gifts are from divine power OR from God.*

Instructor: Does the nightingale decide to eat the worm or to let him go?
Student: *He decides to let him go.*

Ask, "What is one thing you remember about the passage?" Write the student's answer down on the "Instructor" lines of Student Page 124 as he watches. This answer can be the same as one of the answers above.

Now ask the student to copy the sentence in pencil on the "Student" lines below the model. He should attempt to complete the entire sentence.

WEEK 32

Day One: Copywork

Student Page 125

Focus: *Commands*

Pull out Student Page 125. Ask the student to write her name and the date on the correct lines.
The following two model sentences are already printed on it:

Come now and deal the stroke.
Take now the axe and let us see how well you can smite.

Explain to the student that these sentences are from "Sir Gawain and the Green Knight," in which a mysterious knight visits the court of King Arthur during the weeklong Christmas Feast. This knight issues a challenge to any one of King Arthur's knights to take an axe and swing it at him, and these sentences are commands from the knight to accept the challenge.

Tell the student that a command is a sentence that begins with a capital letter and ends with a period, and that also gives an order or makes a request. A statement is another type of sentence that begins with a capital letter and ends with a period, but it gives information; it does not give an order or make a request. Have the student look at both sentences above and ask her to identify the order or the request in each of the two sentences.

Choose whichever sentence is appropriate to the student's handwriting ability. Watch the student as she writes in pencil. If she begins to make an error, gently stop her and ask her to look at the model again.

DAY TWO: Narration Exercise

Student Page 126

Pull out Student Page 126. Ask the student to write her name and the date on the correct lines.

Explain to the student that today's narration comes from *King Arthur and His Knights of the Round Table*, a collection of stories about King Arthur and his royal court. In this story, "Sir Gawain and the Green Knight," a strange man shows up at King Arthur's court during the Christmas Feast, and he presents a challenge to the knights of the court. The following passage tells about his arrival at the court. Tell the student to pay attention to the description of the figure—tell her to listen to the details about what this visitor looks like and what he is wearing, as if she were going to draw a picture of him after the description.

The great doors flew open, and into the hall rode a strange and terrible figure.

A great man it was, riding upon a huge horse: a strong-limbed, great-handed man, so tall that an earth-giant almost he seemed. Yet he rode as a knight should, though without armour, and his face, though fierce, was fair to see—but the greatest wonder was that he was green all over. A jerkin and cloak of green he wore above green hose gartered in green, with golden spurs; in the green belt round his waist jewels were set, and his green saddle was inlaid richly, as were also his trappings. But his hair, hanging low to his shoulders, was bright green, and his beard also; green was his face and green his hands; and the horse was also green from head to foot, with gold thread wound and knotted in the mane.

He had no weapons nor shield save for a great axe of green steel and gold, and a bough torn from a holly tree held above his head. He flung the branch upon the inlaid floor of the hall and looked proudly on every side; at the knights seated about the Round Table, and the ladies and squires at the boards on either side, and at Arthur where he sat with Guinevere above the rest. Then he cried in a great voice:

"Where is the governor of this gang? With him would I speak and with none other!"

All sat in amazement gazing at the strange knight: some dire enchantment it must be, they thought—for how else could there be such a man sitting there on his horse, as green as the grass—greener than any grass on this earth?

But at length Arthur, courteous ever, greeted the Green Knight, bade him be welcome and sit down to the feast with them.

"Not so!" cried the stranger in answer. "I come not to tarry with you: and by the sign of the green bough I come not in war—else had I clothed me in armor and helmet most sure—for such have I richly stored in my castle in the north. But even in that land have I heard of the fame and valor of your court—the bravery of your knights, and their high virtue also."

"Sir," replied the king, "here may you find many to do battle and joust if such be your will."

"Not so," cried the Green Knight in his great booming voice. "Here I see only beardless children whom I could fell with a stroke! Nay, I come rather in this high season of Our Lord's birth to bring Yule-tide sport, a test of valor to your feast."

—From *King Arthur and His Knights of the Round Table*
by Roger Lancelyn Green

Ask the following questions. Remind the student to answer you in complete sentences. If she answers in a fragment, turn the fragment into a complete sentence, say it to her, and then ask her to repeat this sentence back to you. If she cannot answer a question, read her the part of the passage that contains the answer, and then ask the question again.

Instructor: Into the hall rode a strong man. On what kind of animal was he riding?
Student: *He came riding in on a horse.*

Instructor: The knight was strong, fierce, and fair. But what was the most unusual, or striking, thing about him?
Student: *He was green all over!*

Instructor: What were laid into the green belt around the Green Knight's waist?
Student: *The man had jewels inlaid in his belt.*

Instructor: What color was the man's hair? What color was his beard?
Student: *His hair and his beard were green.*

Instructor: Was the man carrying a shield?
Student: *No, he had no shield.*

Instructor: He was carrying one weapon. Can you remember what it was?
Student: *He carried an axe.*

Instructor: The Green Knight wanted to speak with one person. Can you remember who it was?
Student: *He said he wanted to speak with King Arthur OR with the "governor of the gang."*

Instructor: Arthur invited the Green Knight to feast with them. Did he accept?
Student: *No, he did not.*

Instructor: The Green Knight did not come to joust either. What did he say he came to do?
Student: *He said he came to bring a test of valor to the knights of the court.*

Ask, "What is one thing you remember about the passage?" Write the student's answer down on Student Page 126 as she watches. This answer can be the same as one of the answers above.

Day Three: Copywork   *Student Page 127*

Focus: Commands

Pull out Student Page 127. Ask the student to write her name and the date on the correct lines. The following model sentences are already printed on it:

> Noble uncle, let this adventure be mine.
> See to it that you keep your oath and seek me out a year hence.

Explain to the student that these sentences are adapted from "Sir Gawain and the Green Knight." The first sentence is from Sir Gawain, and it is addressed to King Arthur; the second sentence is from the Green Knight, and it is addressed to Sir Gawain.

Remind the student that a command is a sentence that begins with a capital letter and ends with a period, and that also gives an order or makes a request. Have the student look at both sentences above and ask her to identify the order or the request in each of the two sentences.

Choose whichever sentence is appropriate to the student's handwriting ability. Watch the student as she writes in pencil. If she begins to make an error, gently stop her and ask her to look at the model again.

Day Four: Narration Exercise and Copywork   *Student Page 128*

Pull out Student Page 128. Ask the student to write her name and the date on the correct lines.

Explain to the student that the Green Knight made a challenge to any knight in King Arthur's court brave enough to accept. The Green Knight's challenge was this: any one knight could take one swing at him with the axe, as long as that knight would allow him—the Green Knight—to take a swing at his neck one year later. Everyone in the court was silent after they heard the challenge, and King Arthur was about to accept the challenge when one of his bravest knights stood up instead.

You may need to explain that another word for "boon" is "blessing." Also, the word "Logres" is another word for England.

> But at this Sir Gawain rose to his feet and said:
>
> "My lord king and noble uncle, grant me a boon! Let this adventure be mine, for still there is my old shame unhealed: still have I to prove my worth as a knight of your Round Table, still to fit myself to be a champion of Logres."
>
> "Right happy I am that the quest shall be yours, dear nephew," answered Arthur. And the Green Knight smiled grimly as he sprang from his horse and met with Gawain in the middle of the hall.
>
> "I too am overjoyed to find one brave man amongst you all," he said. "Tell me your name, Sir knight, ere we make our bargain."
>
> "I am Gawain, son of King Lot of Orkney, and nephew to royal Arthur," was the answer. "And here I swear by my knighthood to strike but one blow, and bravely to endure such another if you may strike it me a twelve-month hence."
>
> "Sir Gawain," cried the Green Knight, "overjoyed I am indeed that your hand shall strike this blow. Come now and deal the stroke: thereafter shall I tell you who I am and where you may find me. Take now the axe and let us see how well you can smite."
>
> "Gladly will I," said Gawain, taking the axe in his hands and swinging it while the Green Knight made ready by kneeling on the floor and drawing his long hair on the crown of his head to lay bare his neck for the stroke. Putting all his strength into the blow, Gawain whirled up the axe and struck so hard that the keen blade cut through flesh and bone and set the sparks flying from the stone paving, while the Green Knight's head leapt from his shoulders and went rolling across the floor.
>
> But the knight neither faltered nor fell: swiftly he sprang forward with his hands outstretched, caught up his head, and turning with it held in his hand by the hair mounted upon the waiting horse. Then, riding easily as if nothing had happened, he turned his face towards Gawain and said, "See to it that you keep your oath and seek me out a year hence. I am the Knight of the Green Chapel, and as such men know me in the north."
>
> —From *King Arthur and His Knights of the Round Table*
> by Roger Lancelyn Green

Ask the following questions. Remind the student to answer you in complete sentences. If she answers in a fragment, turn the fragment into a complete sentence, say it to her, and then ask her to repeat this sentence back to you. If she cannot answer a question, read her the part of the passage that contains the answer, and then ask the question again.

Instructor: A knight stands up to ask Arthur to accept the challenge. Can you remember the knight's name?
Student: *His name is Sir Gawain.*

Instructor: Does Arthur allow Sir Gawain to accept the challenge?
Student: *Yes, he does.*

Instructor: What does the Green Knight do when Sir Gawain accepts the challenge?
Student: *The Green Knight gets down from his horse and asks his name.*

Instructor: Sir Gawain introduces himself. He then promises the Green Knight two things. Can you remember what they are?
Student: *He promises to deal one blow, and to allow the Green Knight to strike a blow one year later.*

Instructor: The Green Knight says that Sir Gawain should get ready to deal the stroke. After Sir Gawain has done this, the Green Knight will tell him something. Can you remember what it is?
Student: *The Green Knight says that after Sir Gawain deals the stroke, he will tell him who he is and where he can be found a year later.*

Instructor: Sir Gawain deals a strong blow and is able to cut off the Green Knight's head. What happens then?
Student: *The Green Knight gets up and picks up his head and gets on his horse!*

Instructor: What does the Green Knight say to Sir Gawain after he gets on his horse?
Student: *He tells him to come find him in one year, and that he is the Knight of the Green Chapel.*

Ask, "What is one thing you remember about the passage?" Write the student's answer down on the "Instructor" lines of Student Page 128 as she watches. This answer can be the same as one of the answers above.

Now ask the student to copy the sentence in pencil on the "Student" lines below the model. She should attempt to complete the entire sentence.

WEEK 33

DAY ONE: Copywork   *Student Page 129*

Focus: *Questions*

Pull out Student Page 129. Ask the student to write his name and the date on the correct lines. The following two model sentences are already printed on it:

Have I ever told you about Willy Wonka?
Is it true that his chocolate factory is the biggest in the world?

Explain to the student that these sentences are adapted from *Charlie and the Chocolate Factory*, which tells the story of a young boy named Charlie who wins a tour of a top-secret chocolate factory run by Mr. Willy Wonka.

Tell the student that a question is a sentence that begins with a capital letter and ends with a question mark, and that also asks something. Have the student point out the question mark in each of the sentences. Ask him to practice making question marks at the bottom of Student Page 129.

Choose whichever sentence is appropriate to the student's handwriting ability. Watch the student as he writes in pencil. If he begins to make an error, gently stop him and ask him to look at the model again.

DAY TWO: Narration Exercise   *Student Page 130*

Pull out Student Page 130. Ask the student to write his name and the date on the correct lines.

Charlie and the Chocolate Factory tells the story of a young boy named Charlie Bucket who wins a tour of a top-secret chocolate factory run by Mr. Willy Wonka. Charlie lives in a small house with his parents and four grandparents. The following passage introduces the reader to what life is like for Charlie's grandparents.

In the evenings, after he had finished his supper of watery cabbage soup, Charlie always went into the room of his four grandparents to listen to their stories, and then afterwards to say good night.

Every one of these old people was over ninety. They were as shriveled as prunes, and bony as skeletons, and throughout the day, until Charlie made his appearance, they lay huddled in their one bed, two at either end, with nightcaps on to keep their heads warm, dozing the time away with nothing to do. But as soon as they heard the door opening, and heard Charlie's voice saying, "Good evening, Grandpa Joe and Grandma Josephine, and Grandpa George and Grandma Georgina," then all four of them would suddenly sit up, and their old wrinkled faces would light up with smiles of pleasure—and the talking would begin. For they loved this little boy. He was the only bright thing in their lives, and his evening visits were something that they looked forward to all day long. Often, Charlie's mother and father would come in as well, and stand by the door, listening to the stories that the old people told; and thus, for perhaps half an hour every night, this room would become a happy place, and the whole family would forget that it was hungry and poor.

One evening, when Charlie went in to see his grandparents, he said to them, "Is it really true that Wonka's Chocolate factory is the biggest in the world?"

"True?" cried all four of them at once. "Of course it's true! Good heavens, didn't you know that? It's about fifty times as big as any other!"

—From *Charlie and the Chocolate Factory*
by Roald Dahl

Ask the following questions. Remind the student to answer you in complete sentences. If he answers in a fragment, turn the fragment into a complete sentence, say it to him, and then ask him to repeat this sentence back to you. If he cannot answer a question, read him the part of the passage that contains the answer, and then ask the question again.

Instructor: What did Charlie have for supper?
Student: He had watery cabbage soup.

Instructor: Charlie's grandparents were old. Can you remember *how* old?
Student: They were all over ninety years old.

Instructor: What did the grandparents do when Charlie would come into their room in the evening?
Student: They would sit up in bed and begin talking with him.

Instructor: Who else would come in during this time, and what happened?
Student: Charlie's parents also came in and listened to the stories, and the family would forget that it was hungry and poor.

Instructor: What did Charlie ask his grandparents about Wonka's chocolate factory?
Student: He asked them if it was the biggest chocolate factory in the world.

Instructor: What did they say to him?
Student: They said that yes, it was the biggest in the world.

Ask, "What is one thing you remember about the passage?" Write the student's answer down on Student Page 130 as he watches. This answer can be the same as one of the answers above.

DAY THREE: Copywork   *Student Page 131*

Focus: *Questions*

Pull out Student Page 131. Ask the student to write his name and the date on the correct lines. The following model sentences are already printed on it:

Did Mr. Wonka do it?
Have you ever seen a single person going into that place or coming out?

Explain to the student that these sentences are adapted from *Charlie and the Chocolate Factory.* In the above questions, Charlie is talking with his grandparents about the chocolate factory.

Remind the student that a question is a sentence that begins with a capital letter and ends with a question mark, and that also asks something. Have the student point out the question mark in each of the sentences. If he needs it, ask the student to practice making question marks at the bottom of Student Page 131.

Choose whichever sentence is appropriate to the student's handwriting ability. Watch the student as he writes in pencil. If he begins to make an error, gently stop him and ask him to look at the model again.

DAY FOUR: Narration Exercise and Copywork   *Student Page 132*

Pull out Student Page 132. Ask the student to write his name and the date on the correct lines.

Read the following passage out loud to the student. Charlie has not yet heard the stories about Willy Wonka and his chocolate factory, and in the following passage, we see his grandparents as they enjoy telling Charlie all about the inventive chocolate maker.

Grandpa Joe was the oldest of the four grandparents. He was ninety-six and a half, and that is just about as old as anybody can be. Like all extremely old people, he was delicate and weak, and throughout the day he spoke very little. But in the evenings, when Charlie, his beloved grandson, was in the room, he seemed in some marvelous way to grow quite young again. All his tiredness fell away from him, and he became as eager and excited as a young boy.

"Oh, what a man he is, this Mr. Willy Wonka!" cried Grandpa Joe. "Did you know, for example, that he has himself invented more than two hundred new kinds of chocolate bars, each with a different center, each far sweeter and creamier and more delicious than anything the other chocolate factories can make!"

"Perfectly true!" cried Grandma Josephine. "And he sends them to all the four corners of the earth! Isn't that so, Grandpa Joe?"

"It is, my dear, it is. And to all the kings and the presidents of the world as well. But it isn't only chocolate bars that he makes. Oh, dear me, no! He has some really fantastic inventions up his sleeve, Mr. Willy Wonka has! Did you know that he's invented a way of making chocolate ice cream so that it stays cold for hours and hours without being in the refrigerator? You can even leave it lying in the sun all morning on a hot day and it won't go runny!"

"But that's impossible!" said little Charlie, staring at his grandfather.

"Of course it's impossible!" cried Grandpa Joe. "It's completely absurd! But Mr. Willy Wonka has done it."

—From *Charlie and the Chocolate Factory*
by Roald Dahl

Ask the following questions. Remind the student to answer you in complete sentences. If he answers in a fragment, turn the fragment into a complete sentence, say it to him, and then ask him to repeat this sentence back to you. If he cannot answer a question, read him the part of the passage that contains the answer, and then ask the question again.

Instructor: Grandpa Joe was the oldest of the grandparents. How old was Grandpa Joe?
Student: *Grandpa Joe was ninety-six and a half.*

Instructor: What was Grandpa Joe like when he was around his grandson, Charlie?
Student: *He seemed to get young again, and he became excited OR He had more energy.*

Instructor: What did Grandpa Joe tell Charlie about Willy Wonka and chocolate?
Student: *He told Charlie that Mr. Willy Wonka had invented more than two hundred new kinds of chocolate bars.*

Instructor: Grandpa Joe says that Willy Wonka has sent his chocolate bars to some important people of the world. Can you remember one important group of people that receives chocolate bars from Willy Wonka?
Student: *Grandpa Joe says that Willy Wonka has sent his chocolate bars to all the kings and presidents of the world.*

Instructor: Besides chocolate bars, what do the grandparents say that Willy Wonka makes?
Student: *They say he's invented a way to make chocolate ice cream so that it stays cold for hours without being refrigerated!*

Ask, "What is one thing you remember about the passage?" Write the student's answer down on the "Instructor" lines of Student Page 132 as he watches. This answer can be the same as one of the answers above.

Now ask the student to copy the sentence in pencil on the "Student" lines below the model. He should attempt to complete the entire sentence.

WEEK 34

Day One: Copywork   *Student Page 133*

Focus: *Exclamations*

Pull out Student Page 133. Ask the student to write her name and the date on the correct lines. The following two model sentences are already printed on it:

Mommy, he hit me!
Okay, you win this time, but next time, look out!

Explain to the student that these sentences are from *Socks,* which follows the adventures of a black-and-white cat named Socks. When he is just a kitten, Socks narrowly avoids being sold to a child who is complaining to his mother in the first sentence above. In the second sentence, Socks's owner, Mr. Bricker, is yelling at Socks after he has taken some food off the counter.

Tell the student that an exclamation is a sentence that begins with a capital letter and ends with an exclamation point. An exclamation shows sudden or strong feeling. Have the student point out the exclamation point in each of the sentences. Ask her to practice making exclamation points at the bottom of Student Page 133.

Choose whichever sentence is appropriate to the student's handwriting ability. Watch the student as she writes in pencil. If she begins to make an error, gently stop her and ask her to look at the model again.

DAY TWO: Narration Exercise   *Student Page 134*

Pull out Student Page 134. Ask the student to write her name and the date on the correct lines.

Explain to the student that today's narration comes from *Socks,* by Beverly Cleary. A boy, George, and his younger sister, Debbie, have a kitten sale in front of a local food market. Their favorite kitten, Socks, is a small black-and-white tabby, and they want him to go to a good home. A mother and her three poorly behaved children come to buy Socks. George has to think quickly to save him from the children, and he puts Socks in a mailbox nearby.

> Socks had almost wiggled free when a second pair of hands seized him. He felt himself being lifted. Metal creaked, the hands thrust him into the darkness and he found himself falling. He landed on something smooth in a dark, stifling place. Above he heard a creak and a clang. Outside he heard shouting and the sound of Debbie's bursting into tears. The strangest things had happened to Socks that morning.
>
> "He mailed him!" cried the small boy. "That big boy mailed the kitten I wanted."
>
> "The one I wanted," contradicted his big sister.
>
> "Cut it out, you kids," said the mother.
>
> The little sister shrieked, "Mommy, he hit me!" Now she had her brother in the wrong.
>
> Socks slipped and slid on the letters that crackled beneath his paws as he explored the dark mailbox. The place was sweltering, but it was free from other kittens. For the first time in seven weeks of life Socks had found a place where no one could step on his face or bite his tail. He lay down on the letters to catch up on the rest he had missed that morning.
>
> Outside the commotion continued. "I'm fed up with you kids fighting all the time," said the mother. "Just for that we won't buy a kitten at all."
>
> All three children protested. "No fair! You said you'd buy us a kitten. You promised! Please, Mommy. Just one. We won't fight anymore. Honest."

"Come along," said the mother, relieved to have an excuse for leaving the kitten behind. "I'll buy you popsicles instead…"

This decision was followed by shouts of, "I want lime! I want grape!" "I don't want a popsicle! I want a slurpy."

Socks was discovering that the heat inside the box made sleep impossible. The chute at the top opened. "Socks, are you all right down there?" Socks recognized the tearful voice as Debbie's even though it sounded loud and hollow. Then she demanded of her brother, "How are we going to get him out? He'll roast if we leave him in there. He'll starve. He'll die!" She tried to cool the box by opening and closing the creaky chute.

—From *Socks*
by Beverly Cleary

Ask the following questions. Remind the student to answer you in complete sentences. If she answers in a fragment, turn the fragment into a complete sentence, say it to her, and then ask her to repeat this sentence back to you. If she cannot answer a question, read her the part of the passage that contains the answer, and then ask the question again.

Instructor: Socks was trying to wiggle free from one of the three children, when he felt George's hands pick him up. Did Socks know where George was putting him?
Student: *No, he did not.*

Instructor: Outside the mailbox, Socks heard someone burst into tears. Who was it?
Student: *Debbie burst into tears.*

Instructor: What did one of the boys say that George had done?
Student: *He said that George had mailed Socks.*

Instructor: What was Socks walking on top of while he was in the mailbox?
Student: *He was walking on top of the letters that were in the mailbox.*

Instructor: Was it hot or cool inside the mailbox?
Student: *It was very hot inside the mailbox.*

Instructor: The mother of the three children did not decide to take another kitten instead. What did she decide to do?
Student: *She decided not to buy a kitten at all, but to buy popsicles for the children.*

Instructor: Socks wasn't able to fall asleep in the mailbox. Can you remember why?
Student: *It was too hot to sleep.*

Instructor: How did Debbie try to cool the inside of the mailbox?
Student: *She tried to cool the mailbox by opening and closing the chute.*

Ask, "What is one thing you remember about the passage?" Write the student's answer down on Student Page 134 as she watches. This answer can be the same as one of the answers above.

DAY THREE: Copywork

Focus: *Exclamations*

Pull out Student Page 135. Ask the student to write her name and the date on the correct lines. The following model sentences are already printed on it:

> Mommy, Socks likes me!
> My, you are a big handsome boy with a nice thick coat!

Explain to the student that these sentences are from *Socks,* by Beverly Cleary. In the sentences above, Socks finds attention from a neighborhood girl and from a babysitter.

Remind the student that an exclamation is a sentence that begins with a capital letter and ends with an exclamation point. An exclamation shows sudden or strong feeling. Have the student point out the exclamation point in each of the sentences. Ask her to practice making exclamation points at the bottom of Student Page 135.

Choose whichever sentence is appropriate to the student's handwriting ability. Watch the student as she writes in pencil. If she begins to make an error, gently stop her and ask her to look at the model again.

DAY FOUR: Narration Exercise and Copywork

Pull out Student Page 136. Ask the student to write her name and the date on the correct lines.

Explain to the student that Socks was soon rescued from the mailbox. He was then bought by a nice young couple, Mr. and Mrs. Bricker. Socks adjusted to and loved his life with this couple. In the following passage, Socks has been waiting for Mr. and Mrs. Bricker to come home. They've been away for a few days, though he doesn't know they've gone to the hospital to have a baby. He hears the car pulling in, and he looks forward to their arrival home.

> "Did you miss me, Socks?" Mrs. Bricker stooped to rub the hollow behind his ears where his fur grew short and fine. "Were you lonesome without me?" she asked.
> Socks's throat pulsated with purrs. He rubbed against her legs, back and forth, round and round, as she entered the house. He could not get enough petting to satisfy his pent-up loneliness.
> "I missed you, too," said Mrs. Bricker in such an understanding voice that Socks felt he must take advantage of her. With a hopeful meow, he started toward the kitchen, paused, and looked back to encourage her to follow him to the refrigerator. Until that moment he had been so happy to see his family that he had not noticed the bundle in Mr. Bricker's arms.
> Socks hesitated. Which was more important, a tidbit from the refrigerator or his right to investigate everything that came into the house? Curiosity won, and he turned back.

"See what we've brought," said Mr. Bricker.

A smacking noise came from inside the bundle. Instantly Socks was alert. There was something alive in there. His spine prickled, and he paused to sniff cautiously.

Mrs. Bricker folded back the blanket, and Mr. Bricker leaned over so Socks could see. He saw a creature with a small, wrinkled, furless face, a sight that made his hair stand on end. His eyes grew large and he back away. Whatever the thing was, he did not trust it.

As Socks stared at the strange creature in the bundle and listened to it smack and snuffle, he began to understand. His owners, his faithful, loving owners, had brought home a new pet to threaten his position in the household. Socks turned his back and lashed his swollen tail. He was filled with jealousy and anger and a terrible anxiety. The Brickers might love the new pet more than they loved him.

—From *Socks*
by Beverly Cleary

Ask the following questions. Remind the student to answer you in complete sentences. If she answers in a fragment, turn the fragment into a complete sentence, say it to her, and then ask her to repeat this sentence back to you. If she cannot answer a question, read her the part of the passage that contains the answer, and then ask the question again.

Instructor: When Mrs. Bricker comes home, what does she ask Socks?
Student: She asks if Socks has missed her.

Instructor: What does Socks do that lets you know that he has missed Mrs. Bricker?
Student: Socks purrs and rubs against her legs.

Instructor: Socks hopes to lead Mrs. Bricker to the kitchen. What is he hoping for?
Student: He is hoping for a tidbit from the refrigerator.

Instructor: In his hope for a treat from the refrigerator, what does Socks not notice?
Student: He doesn't notice the bundle in Mr. Bricker's arms.

Instructor: After he realizes that the bundle is alive, what does he do?
Student: His spine prickles, and he sniffs cautiously.

Instructor: Does Socks trust this new creature?
Student: No, he does not.

Instructor: What does Socks begin to understand about what his owners have done?
Student: He begins to understand that they have brought home a new pet.

Instructor: Does Socks react to this new "pet" with love and affection, or with anger and jealousy?
Student: He reacts with anger and jealousy.

Ask, "What is one thing you remember about the passage?" Write the student's answer down on the "Instructor" lines of Student Page 136 as she watches. This answer can be the same as one of the answers above.

Now ask the student to copy the sentence in pencil on the "Student" lines below the model. She should attempt to complete the entire sentence.

WEEK 35

Day One: Copywork   *Student Page 137*

Focus: *Review questions*

Pull out Student Page 137. Ask the student to write his name and the date on the correct lines. The following two model sentences are already printed on it:

> Is the river so nice as all that?
> If you have nothing else on hand this morning, supposing we drop down the river together, and have a long day of it?

Explain to the student that these sentences are adapted from *The Wind and the Willows*, in which four friends—Rat, Mole, Badger, and Toad—have adventures together. Mole is asking Rat about the river in the first sentence above; in the second sentence, Rat invites Mole to go for a boat ride on the river.

Remind the student that a question is a sentence that begins with a capital letter and ends with a question mark, and that also asks something. Have the student point out the question mark in each of the sentences. If he needs it, ask the student to practice making question marks at the bottom of Student Page 137.

Choose whichever sentence is appropriate to the student's handwriting ability. Watch the student as he writes in pencil. If he begins to make an error, gently stop him and ask him to look at the model again.

Day Two: Narration Exercise   *Student Page 138*

Pull out Student Page 138. Ask the student to write his name and the date on the correct lines.

The Wind in the Willows follows the adventures of Rat, Mole, Badger, and Toad. Mole has just finished cleaning his house and comes out for his first-ever look at the river. Mole sees Rat, who spends most of his time on the river and knows it well. Rat is on one side of the river, and Mole is on the other.

"Would you like to come over?" enquired the Rat presently.

"Oh, it's all very well to *talk*," said the Mole, rather pettishly, he being new to a river and riverside life and its ways.

The Rat said nothing, but stooped and unfastened a rope and hauled on it; then lightly stepped into a little boat which the Mole had not observed. It was painted blue outside and white within, and was just the size for two animals; and the Mole's whole heart went out to it at once, even though he did not yet fully understand its uses.

The Rat sculled smartly across and made fast. Then he held up his forepaw as the Mole stepped gingerly down. "Lean on that!" he said. "Now then, step lively!" and the Mole to his surprise and rapture found himself actually seated in the stern of a real boat.

"This has been a wonderful day!" said he, as the Rat shoved off and took to the sculls again.

"Do you know, I've never been in a boat before in all my life."

"What?" cried the Rat, open-mouthed: "Never been in a—you never—well I—what have you been doing, then?"

"Is it so nice as all that?" asked the Mole shyly, though he was quite prepared to believe it as he leant back in his seat and surveyed the cushions, the oars, the rowlocks, and all the fascinating fittings, and felt the boat sway lightly under him.

"Nice? It's the *only* thing," said the Water Rat solemnly, as he leant forward for his stroke. "Believe me, my young friend, there is *nothing*—absolutely nothing—half so much worth doing as simply messing about in boats. Simply messing," he went on dreamily: "messing—about—in—boats; messing—"

"Look ahead, Rat!" cried the Mole suddenly.

It was too late. The boat struck the bank full tilt. The dreamer, the joyous oarsman, lay on his back at the bottom of the boat, his heels in the air.

—From *The Wind in the Willows*
by Kenneth Grahame

Ask the following questions. Remind the student to answer you in complete sentences. If he answers in a fragment, turn the fragment into a complete sentence, say it to him, and then ask him to repeat this sentence back to you. If he cannot answer a question, read him the part of the passage that contains the answer, and then ask the question again.

Instructor: What does Rat ask Mole if he would like to do?
Student: *He asks him if he'd like to come over.*

Instructor: Rat then unties a rope and steps down into something that Mole has not yet seen. Can you remember what it was?
Student: *Rat steps down into a little boat.*

Instructor: Can you remember the two colors the boat is painted?
Student: *The boat is painted blue outside, and it is white on the inside.*

Instructor: Rat takes the boat across the river and helps Mole into the boat. Has the Mole ever been in a boat before?
Student: *No; this is his first time.*

Instructor: Mole looks around the boat. Can you remember one of the things that he notices in the boat?
Student: *He looks at the oars, the rowlocks, the cushions, and the fittings in the boat.*

Instructor: Rat rows dreamily along, and Mole calls to him to look out. What does the boat crash into?
Student: *The boat crashes into the bank.*

Ask, "What is one thing you remember about the passage?" Write the student's answer down on Student Page 138 as he watches. This answer can be the same as one of the answers above.

DAY THREE: Copywork   *Student Page 139*

Focus: *Review exclamations*

Pull out Student Page 139. Ask the student to write his name and the date on the correct lines. The following model sentences are already printed on it:

> This has been a wonderful day!
> How black was his despair when he felt himself sinking again!

Ask the student to look carefully at the sentences. While he is examining them, explain that both are from *The Wind in the Willows.* Mole enjoys his day on the river with Rat, though he has a brief scare when he falls out of the boat. Not knowing how to swim, Mole is grateful when Rat pulls him to safety.

Remind the student that an exclamation is a sentence that begins with a capital letter and ends with an exclamation point. An exclamation shows sudden or strong feeling. Have the student point out the exclamation point in each of the sentences. If he needs it, ask him to practice making exclamation points at the bottom of Student Page 139.

Choose whichever sentence is appropriate to the student's handwriting ability. Watch the student as he writes in pencil. If he begins to make an error, gently stop him and ask him to look at the model again.

DAY FOUR: Narration Exercise and Copywork   *Student Page 140*

Pull out Student Page 140. Ask the student to write his name and the date on the correct lines.

Read the following passage out loud to the student. Explain that Rat and Mole are returning from a picnic when Mole decides that he wants to do the rowing. Rat politely says no, but when Mole grabs the oars out of Rat's hands, the boat turns over and both of them get wet. Mole apologizes for his poor behavior.

You may need to explain that Toad is the wealthiest of the creatures, and has the nicest house at Toad Hall. A "weir" is a dam-like structure, and a "pike" is a long fish with a pointy head and sharp teeth.

"That's all right, bless you!" responded the Rat cheerily. "What's a little wet to a Water Rat? I'm more in the water than out of it most days. Don't you think any more about it; and, look here! I really think you had better come and stop with me for a little time. It's very plain and rough, you know—not like Toad's house at all—but you haven't seen that yet; still, I can make you comfortable. And I'll teach you to row, and to swim, and you'll soon be as handy on the water as any of us."

The Mole was so touched by his kind manner of speaking that he could find no voice to answer him; and he had to brush away a tear or two with the back of his paw. But the Rat kindly looked in another direction, and presently the Mole's spirits revived again, and he was even able to give some straight back-talk to a couple of moorhens who were sniggering to each other about his bedraggled appearance.

When they got home, the Rat made a bright fire in the parlour, and planted the Mole in an arm-chair in front of it, having fetched down a dressing-gown and slippers for him, and told him river stories till supper-time. Very thrilling stories they were, too, to an earth-dwelling animal like Mole. Stories about weirs, and sudden floods, and leaping pike, and steamers that flung hard bottles—at least bottles were certainly flung, and *from* steamers, so presumably *by* them; and about herons, and how particular they were whom they spoke to; and about adventures down drains, and night-fishings with Otter, or excursions far a-field with Badger. Supper was a most cheerful meal; but very shortly afterwards a terribly sleepy Mole had to be escorted upstairs by his considerate host, to the best bedroom, where he soon laid his head on his pillow in great peace and contentment, knowing that his new-found friend the River was lapping the sill of his window.

This day was only the first of many similar ones for the emancipated Mole, each of them longer and full of interest as the ripening summer moved onward. He learnt to swim and to row, and entered into the joy of running water; and with his ear to the reed-stems he caught, at intervals, something of what the wind went whispering so constantly among them.

—From *The Wind in the Willows*
by Kenneth Grahame

Ask the following questions. Remind the student to answer you in complete sentences. If he answers in a fragment, turn the fragment into a complete sentence, say it to him, and then ask him to repeat this sentence back to you. If he cannot answer a question, read him the part of the passage that contains the answer, and then ask the question again.

Instructor: Is Rat angry with Mole for getting him wet?
Student: *No, he is not angry with him.*

Instructor: Rat invites Mole to his house, and then he offers to teach him a few things. Can you remember one of them?
Student: *He offers to teach him how to row, and to swim, and to be handy on the water.*

Instructor: When they get home, what does Rat do to warm them up?
Student: *He builds a fire.*

Instructor: What do both of them do around the fire, before dinner?
Student: *Rat tells stories, and Mole listens to them.*

Instructor: Can you remember one of the other characters that Rat mentions in his stories?
Student: *He mentions Otter and Badger.*

Instructor: Mole spends the night in the best bedroom. What is lapping just outside his window?
Student: *The river is lapping just outside his bedroom window.*

Instructor: Does Mole eventually learn to swim and to row from Rat?
Student: *Yes, he does learn to swim and to row.*

Ask, "What is one thing you remember about the passage?" Write the student's answer down on the "Instructor" lines of Student Page 140 as he watches. This answer can be the same as one of the answers above.

Now ask the student to copy the sentence in pencil on the "Student" lines below the model. He should attempt to complete the entire sentence.

WEEK 36

Mastery Evaluation

This week's assignments are designed to evaluate the student's mastery of the Level One skills. Before moving to Level Two, the student should be able to copy a ten-word sentence without error, accurately answer questions about a three- to five-paragraph passage, and answer the question "What is one thing you remember about the passage?" with a complete sentence.

Feel free to give some help, but if the student is frustrated by with any of these assignments, spend some additional time working on copywork or narration before moving on to Level Two.

DAY ONE: Copywork   *Student Page 141*

Pull out Evaluation Page 1 (Student page 141). Ask the student to write her name and the date on the correct lines.

The following model sentences are already printed on it:

> The rain is falling all around,
> It falls on field and tree,
> It rains on the umbrellas here,
> And on the ships at sea.
>
> —From *A Child's Garden of Verses*
> by Robert Lois Stevenson

Tell the student that poem is called "Rain." Ask the student to copy them out in her own handwriting below the model. Remind the student that her copy should look exactly like the model, but do not give other specific suggestions.

If the student misspells more than one word and does not reproduce the punctuation and capitalization properly, spend a few more weeks on copywork before moving on to Level Two.

DAY TWO: Narration Exercise   *Student Page 142*

Pull out Evaluation Page 2 (Student page 142). Ask the student to write her name and the date on the correct lines.

Tell the student that this excerpt is from the beginning of *The Wonderful Wizard of Oz,* by L. Frank Baum. In this story, a little girl named Dorothy is picked up by a cyclone (a tornado) and taken to a magical country called Oz. Toto is Dorothy's little dog.

> From the far north they heard a low wail of the wind, and Uncle Henry and Dorothy could see where the long grass bowed in waves before the coming storm. There now came a sharp whistling in the air from the south, and as they turned their eyes that way they saw ripples in the grass coming from that direction also.
>
> Suddenly Uncle Henry stood up.
>
> "There's a cyclone coming, Em," he called to his wife. "I'll go look after the stock." Then he ran toward the sheds where the cows and horses were kept.
>
> Aunt Em dropped her work and came to the door. One glance told her of the danger close at hand.
>
> "Quick, Dorothy!" she screamed. "Run for the cellar!"
>
> Toto jumped out of Dorothy's arms and hid under the bed, and the girl started to get him. Aunt Em, badly frightened, threw open the trap door in the floor and climbed down the ladder into the small, dark hole. Dorothy caught Toto at last and started to follow her aunt. When she was halfway

across the room there came a great shriek from the wind, and the house shook so hard that she lost her footing and sat down suddenly upon the floor.

Then a strange thing happened.

The house whirled around two or three times and rose slowly through the air. Dorothy felt as if she were going up in a balloon.

The north and south winds met where the house stood, and made it the exact center of the cyclone. In the middle of a cyclone the air is generally still, but the great pressure of the wind on every side of the house raised it up higher and higher, until it was at the very top of the cyclone; and there it remained and was carried miles and miles away as easily as you could carry a feather.

—From *The Wonderful Wizard of Oz*
by L. Frank Baum

Ask the following questions. The student may need to be prompted for the answer to one of the questions that follow, but if she doesn't know the answers to two or three of the questions, she should practice listening on more passages of this length before going on to Level Two.

You may need to remind the student to answer in complete sentences, but you should not have to form the complete sentences for her. If so, she needs additional practice before going on to Level Two.

Instructor: What are the names of Dorothy's uncle and aunt?
Student: *They are named Uncle Henry and Aunt Em.*

Instructor: Dorothy and Uncle Henry saw and heard three things that warned them of the coming cyclone. Can you remember one of them?
Student: *They heard the wind wail OR They saw ripples in the grass OR They heard whistling in the air.*

Instructor: Where did Uncle Henry go, after he warned Aunt Em about the cyclone?
Student: *He ran to the sheds where the cows and horses were.*

Instructor: Where did Toto go?
Student: *Toto hid under the bed.*

Instructor: Where did Aunt Em go?
Student: *She went through the trap door in the floor.*

Instructor: What happened to Dorothy and the house?
Student: *They were carried up into the cyclone.*

Ask, "What is one thing you remember about the passage?" Write the student's answer down on Evaluation Page 2 (Student page 142) as she watches.

DAY THREE: Copywork   *Student Page 143*

Pull out Evaluation Page 3 (Student page 143). Ask the student to write his name and the date on the correct lines.

The following model sentences are already printed on it:

> L. Frank Baum wrote stories about a little girl who lived in Kansas. Her name was Dorothy, and she went to the land of Oz.

Ask the student to copy both sentences onto the lines below the model. Remind the student that the copied sentences should look exactly like the original, but do not give any other specific reminders.

If the student misspells more than one word and does not reproduce the punctuation and capitalization properly, spend a few more weeks on copywork before moving on to Level Two.

DAY FOUR: Narration Exercise   *Student Page 144*

Pull out Evaluation Page 4 (Student page 144). Ask the student to write his name and the date on the correct lines.

Tell the student that, after Dorothy landed in the land of Oz, she found herself in the land of the Munchkins, peaceful farmers who wore blue. She left the Munchkins to go to the city of Oz, because she thought that the wizard who lived there might be able to help her get back to Kansas.

> She bade her friends good-bye, and again started along the road of yellow brick. When she had gone several miles she thought she would stop to rest, and so climbed to the top of the fence beside the road and sat down. There was a great cornfield beyond the fence,and not far away she saw a Scarecrow, placed high on a pole to keep the birds from the ripe corn.
>
> Dorothy leaned her chin upon her hand and gazed thoughtfully at the Scarecrow. Its head was a small sack stuffed with straw, with eyes, nose, and mouth painted on it to represent a face.
>
> An old, pointed blue hat, that had belonged to some Munchkin, was perched on his head, and the rest of the figure was a blue suit of clothes, worn and faded, which had also been stuffed with straw. On the feet were some old boots with blue tops, such as every man wore in this country, and the figure was raised above the stalks of corn by means of the pole stuck up its back.
>
> While Dorothy was looking earnestly into the queer, painted face of the Scarecrow, she was surprised to see one of the eyes slowly wink at her. She thought she must have been mistaken at first, for none of the scarecrows in Kansas ever wink; but presently the figure nodded its head to her in a

friendly way. Then she climbed down from the fence and walked up to it, while Toto ran around the pole and barked.

"Good day," said the Scarecrow, in a rather husky voice.

"Did you speak?" asked the girl, in wonder.

"Certainly," answered the Scarecrow. "How do you do?"

"I'm pretty well, thank you," replied Dorothy politely. "How do you do?"

"I'm not feeling well," said the Scarecrow, with a smile, "for it is very tedious being perched up here night and day to scare away crows."

—From *The Wonderful Wizard of Oz*
by L. Frank Baum

Ask the following questions. The student may need to be prompted once, but if he doesn't know the answers to two or three of the questions, he should practice his comprehension skills on more passages of this length before going on to Level Two.

You may need to remind the student to answer in complete sentences, but you should not have to form the complete sentences for him. If this is still necessary, he needs additional practice before going on to Level Two.

Instructor: What kind of road did Dorothy follow?
Student: *She followed a road of yellow brick.*

Instructor: What did she see when she sat on the fence beside the road?
Student: *She saw a Scarecrow.*

Instructor: Why was the Scarecrow in the field?
Student: *He was there to scare the crows away from the crops.*

Instructor: What color was the Scarecrow wearing?
Student: *He was wearing blue.*

Instructor: How did Dorothy know that the Scarecrow was alive?
Student: *He winked at her.*

Instructor: Was the Scarecrow content to be on his pole?
Student: *No; he was bored with scaring crows.*

Ask, "What is one thing you remember about the passage?" Write the student's answer down on the "Instructor" lines of Evaluation Page 4 (Student page 144) as he watches. This answer can be the same as one of the answers above.

Now ask the student to copy the sentence in pencil on the "Student" lines below the model. He should be able to complete the entire sentence at one sitting. If the student misspells more than one word and does not reproduce the punctuation and capitalization properly, spend a few more weeks on copywork before moving on to Level Two.

THE COMPLETE WRITER

Level One
Workbook for Writing with Ease

STUDENT PAGES

By

Susan Wise Bauer

and

Peter Buffington

Peace Hill Press

18021 The Glebe Lane
Charles City, VA 23030
www.peacehillpress.com

$11.95
ISBN 978-1-933339-36-8
51195>

Copywork

There were no roads.

The deer and the rabbits would be shy and swift.

Narration

From *Little House in the Big Woods,* by Laura Ingalls Wilder

What is one thing you remember about the passage?

Copywork

Pa owned a pig.

There was plenty of fresh meat to last for a long time.

Name _____

Narration

From *Little House in the Big Woods*, by Laura Ingalls Wilder

What is one thing you remember about the passage?

_____

- -

_____

- -

_____

- -

_____

- -

_____

- -

_____

- -

_____

- -

_____

- -

_____

Name _____

Geppetto made Pinocchio.

Geppetto decided to make a wooden puppet named
Pinocchio.

Name _____

From *The Adventures of Pinocchio,* by Carlo Collodi

What is one thing you remember about the passage?

_____

_____

_____

_____

_____

_____

_____

_____

_____

_____

_____

_____

_____

_____

_____

_____

The puppet was Pinocchio.

Geppetto made the puppet Pinocchio out of wood.

Narration

From *The Adventures of Pinocchio,* by Carlo Collodi

What is one thing you remember about the passage?

_____

_____

_____

_____

_____

_____

_____

_____

_____

_____

_____

_____

Copywork

A poor miller had a daughter.

_____

- -

_____

- -

_____

- -

_____

Once upon a time a poor miller had a beautiful daughter.

_____

- -

_____

- -

_____

- -

_____

Name _____

Narration

From *The Blue Fairy Book,* by Andrew Lang

What is one thing you remember about the passage?

Date _____

Name _____

Week 3
Day Three

Copywork

His name was Rumpelstiltzkin.

She asked him if his name was Sheepshanks or Cruickshanks.

Name _____

From *The Blue Fairy Book,* by Andrew Lang

What is one thing you remember about the passage?

_____

_____

_____

_____

_____

_____

_____

_____

_____

_____

_____

_____

Alice was silent.

_____

- -

_____

- -

_____

- -

_____

The caterpillar was the first to speak.

_____

- -

_____

- -

_____

- -

_____

Narration

From *Alice's Adventures in Wonderland*, by Lewis Carroll

What is one thing you remember about the passage?

_____

The first witness was the Hatter.

One of the jurors had a pencil that squeaked.

Name _____

Narration and Copywork

From *Alice's Adventures in Wonderland*, by Lewis Carroll

What is one thing you remember about the passage?

Instructor

_____
- -
_____
_____
- -
_____
_____
- -
_____

Student

_____
- -
_____
_____
- -
_____
_____
- -
_____
_____
- -
_____

Copywork

Jacob Grimm wrote down fairy tales.

_____
- -
_____
- -
_____
- -
_____

Jacob Grimm and Wilhelm Grimm were brothers who
collected fairy tales.

_____
- -
_____
_____
- -
_____
_____
- -
_____

Narration

From "The Frog Prince," by Jacob and Wilhelm Grimm

What is one thing you remember about the passage?

_____

Copywork

Edgar Taylor translated the fairy tales.

_____

- -

_____

- -

_____

- -

_____

Edgar Taylor and Marian Edwardes translated the fairy tales into English.

_____

- -

_____

- -

_____

- -

_____

Name _____

Narration and Copywork

From "The Frog Prince," by Jacob and Wilhelm Grimm

What is one thing you remember about the passage?

Instructor

_____

- -

_____

- -

_____

- -

_____

Student

_____

- -

_____

- -

_____

- -

_____

- -

_____

Name _____

Copywork

Jane and Michael Banks stared.

_____
- -
_____
_____
- -
_____
_____
- -
_____

Jane and Michael Banks stared at their new nanny,
Mary Poppins.

_____
- -
_____
_____
- -
_____
_____
- -
_____

Name _____

From *Mary Poppins*, by P. L. Travers

What is one thing you remember about the passage?

_____

- -

_____

_____

- -

_____

_____

- -

_____

_____

- -

_____

_____

- -

_____

_____

- -

_____

_____

- -

_____

Mary Poppins gave Jane and Michael medicine.

Mary Poppins taught Jane and Michael Banks how to say the word supercalifragilisticexpialidocius.

Narration and Copywork

From *Mary Poppins,* by P. L. Travers

What is one thing you remember about the passage?

Instructor

_____

- -

_____

_____

- -

_____

- -

_____

Student

_____

- -

_____

- -

_____

- -

_____

- -

_____

Copywork

Peter Rabbit lived under a fir tree.

_____

- -

_____

_____

- -

_____

_____

- -

_____

Flopsy, Mopsy, and Cottontail were good little bunnies.

_____

- -

_____

_____

- -

_____

_____

- -

_____

Narration

From *The Tale of Peter Rabbit,* by Beatrix Potter

What is one thing you remember about the passage?

_____

Copywork

Beatrix Potter was born in London.

_____

- -

_____

- -

_____

- -

_____

Beatrix Potter was born in London, but she bought a farm
in Sawrey, England.

_____

- -

_____

_____

- -

_____

_____

- -

_____

Name _____

Narration and Copywork

From *The Tale of Peter Rabbit,* by Beatrix Potter

What is one thing you remember about the passage?

Instructor

_____
- -
_____
_____
- -
_____
_____
- -
_____

Student

_____
- -
_____
_____
- -
_____
_____
- -
_____
_____
- -
_____

The Woodlawn family was from Boston.

Caddie Woodlawn and her family moved to the state
of Wisconsin.

Name _____

Narration

From *Caddie Woodlawn,* by Carol Ryrie Brink

What is one thing you remember about the passage?

_____

_____

_____

_____

_____

_____

_____

_____

_____

_____

_____

_____

_____

_____

_____

_____

_____

_____

The circuit rider was from Boston.

The circuit rider rode all over the state of Wisconsin.

Narration and Copywork

From *Caddie Woodlawn,* by Carol Ryrie Brink

What is one thing you remember about the passage?

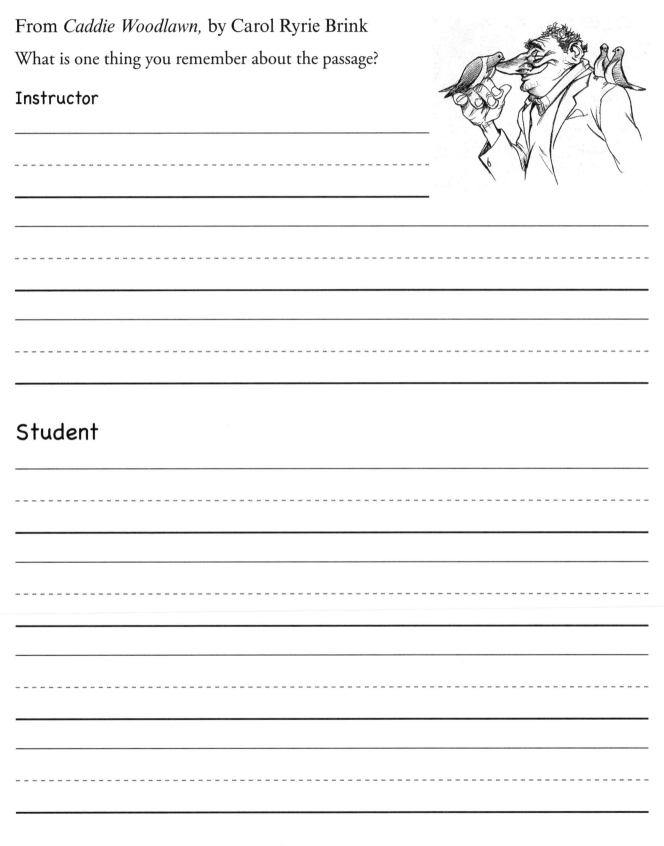

Instructor

_____

- -

_____

_____

- -

_____

_____

- -

_____

Student

_____

- -

_____

_____

- -

_____

_____

- -

_____

_____

- -

_____

The school bus honked from the road.

The teacher asked Fern to name the capital of Pennsylvania.

Narration

From *Charlotte's Web,* by E. B. White

What is one thing you remember about the passage?

_____

_____

_____

_____

_____

_____

_____

_____

_____

_____

_____

_____

_____

_____

_____

Copywork

She named him Wilbur.

Fern took no notice of the others on the bus.

Name _____

Narration and Copywork

From *Charlotte's Web,* by E. B. White

What is one thing you remember about the passage?

Instructor

_____

- -

_____

_____

- -

_____

_____

- -

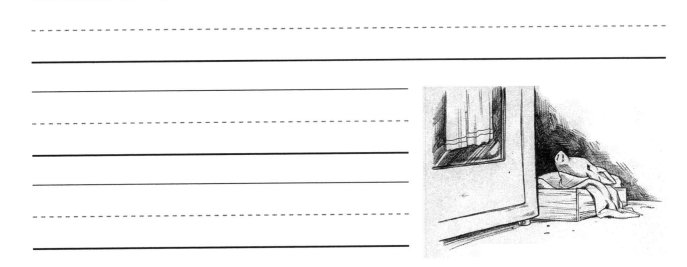

Student

_____

- -

_____

_____

- -

_____

_____

- -

_____

Copywork

Davy Crockett was born in Tennessee.

_____

- -

_____

_____

- -

_____

- -

_____

Davy Crockett lived in Tennessee, but he wanted to explore
the state of Texas.

_____

- -

_____

_____

- -

_____

_____

- -

_____

Narration

From *Davy Crockett, Young Rifleman,* by Aileen Wells Parks

What is one thing you remember about the passage?

_____

_____

_____

_____

_____

_____

_____

_____

_____

_____

_____

_____

Name _____

Sacagawea belonged to the Shoshoni tribe.

Sacagawea helped Meriwether Lewis and William Clark explore the Missouri River.

Date _____

Name _____

Narration and Copywork

From *Sacagawea: American Pathfinder*, by Flora Warren Seymour

What is one thing you remember about the passage?

Instructor

_____

_____

_____

_____

Student

_____

_____

_____

_____

_____

_____

_____

Louis is a musician.

He came here from Montana with Sam Beaver.

Narration

From *The Trumpet of the Swan,* by E. B. White

What is one thing you remember about the passage?

_____

- -

_____

_____

- -

_____

_____

- -

_____

_____

- -

_____

_____

- -

_____

_____

- -

_____

_____

- -

_____

_____

- -

_____

Louis had no trouble finding Philadelphia.

They flew south across Maryland and Virginia.

Date _____

Name _____

Narration and Copywork

From *The Trumpet of the Swan,* by E. B. White

What is one thing you remember about the passage?

Instructor

_____

- -

_____

_____

- -

_____

- -

_____

Student

_____

- -

_____

_____

- -

_____

_____

- -

_____

Copywork

Today is Monday, today is Monday.

Today is Wednesday, today is Wednesday. Wednesday is soup day.

Narration

From "Today Is Monday"

What is one thing you remember about the passage?

_____

- -

_____

- -

_____

- -

_____

- -

_____

- -

_____

- -

_____

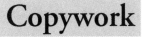

On Thursday we eat roast beef.

_____

- -

_____

- -

_____

- -

_____

Today is Friday. On Friday we clean the house from top to bottom.

_____

- -

_____

_____

- -

_____

_____

- -

_____

Narration and Copywork

From "Old Mother Hubbard", by Anonymous

What is one thing you remember about the passage?

Instructor

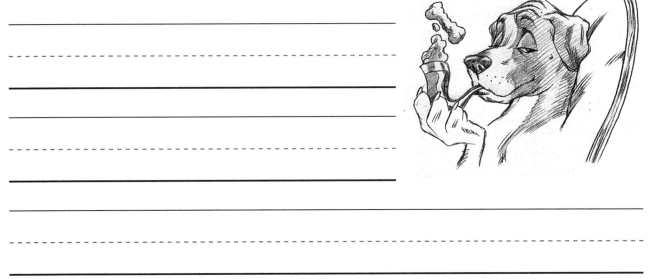

_____

- -

_____

_____

- -

_____

_____

- -

_____

Student

_____

- -

_____

_____

- -

_____

_____

- -

_____

_____

- -

_____

Name _____

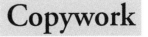

Rain is for Saturday and Sunday.

Good weather is for Monday, Tuesday, Wednesday, Thursday, and Friday.

Narration

From *The Saturdays,* by Elizabeth Enright

What is one thing you remember about the passage?

_____

- -

_____

_____

- -

_____

_____

- -

_____

_____

- -

_____

_____

- -

_____

_____

- -

_____

_____

- -

_____

Copywork

Saturday dawned much the same as any other day.

When Randy woke up, she had the same feeling in her stomach that she always had on Christmas Day.

Name _____

From *The Saturdays,* by Elizabeth Enright

What is one thing you remember about the passage?

Instructor

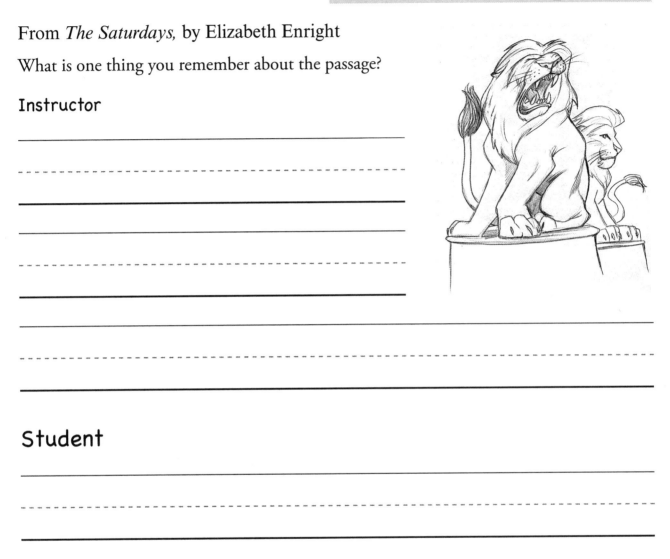

Student

Name _____

Thirty days hath September,
April, June, and November.
All the rest have thirty-one,
Except for February alone.
Which has four and twenty-four,
Til leap year gives it one day more.

The month of December has 31 days.

The months of January, March, August, and October all have 31 days.

Narration

From "Bed in Summer," by Robert Louis Stevenson

Why is the child unhappy?

_____

_____

_____

_____

_____

_____

_____

_____

_____

_____

_____

_____

_____

_____

_____

_____

_____

Name _____

June and July are summer months.

December and January are winter months, but March is a
spring month.

Narration and Copywork

Traditional folk tale, adapted by Susan Wise Bauer

What is one thing you remember about the passage?

Instructor

_____

- -

_____

_____

- -

_____

- -

_____

Student

_____

- -

_____

_____

- -

_____

_____

- -

_____

Copywork

But in June came three wet days.

_____

- -

_____

- -

_____

- -

_____

It was September, and the turf was dry and crisp.

_____

- -

_____

- -

_____

_____

- -

_____

- -

_____

Narration

From *The Railway Children,* by Edith Nesbit

What is one thing you remember about the passage?

_____

_____

_____

_____

_____

_____

_____

_____

_____

_____

_____

_____

_____

_____

But it happened to be a wet day and, for July, very cold.

They had seen the blossom on the trees in the spring, and they knew where to look for wild cherries.

Narration and Copywork

From *The Railway Children,* by Edith Nesbit

What is one thing you remember about the passage?

Instructor

Student

Name _____

Copywork

Today is _____, _____ _____, _____.
               (day of the week)   (month)   (day)   (year)

I was born on _____, _____ _____, _____.
                 (day of the week)   (month)   (day)   (year)

Narration

From "Master of All Masters," folk tale retold by Joseph Jacobs

What is one thing you remember about the passage?

_____

- -

_____

_____

- -

_____

_____

- -

_____

_____

- -

_____

_____

- -

_____

_____

- -

_____

_____

- -

_____

Aesop was a slave who lived in ancient Greece.

Aesop lived on an island called Samos. He once visited Athens, the greatest city in Greece.

Name _____

Narration and Copywork

From "The Dog and His Reflection," by Aesop

What is one thing you remember about the passage?

Instructor

_____

- -

_____

_____

- -

_____

- -

Student

_____

- -

_____

_____

- -

_____

_____

- -

_____

Copywork

You know about sheep, and I know about dragons.

I always said, you know, that that cave up there was a dragon-cave.

Narration

From *The Reluctant Dragon*, by Kenneth Grahame

What is one thing you remember about the passage?

_____

_____

_____

_____

_____

_____

_____

_____

_____

_____

_____

_____

_____

_____

_____

_____

_____

Name _____

You must tell him that I will not fight.

In the old days, I always let the other dragons do all the fighting.

Name _____

From *The Reluctant Dragon,* by Kenneth Grahame

What is one thing you remember about the passage?

Instructor

Student

Copywork

It was a warm day, and he had a long way to go.

Outside his house he found Piglet, jumping up and down trying to reach the knocker.

Narration

From *Winnie-the-Pooh,* by A. A. Milne

What is one thing you remember about the passage?

_____

He dropped his pine cone into the river.

But then he thought he would just look at the river
instead, because it was a peaceful sort of day.

Narration and Copywork

From *The House at Pooh Corner,* by A. A. Milne

What is one thing you remember about the passage?

Instructor

_____

- -

_____

_____

- -

_____

_____

- -

_____

Student

_____

- -

_____

_____

- -

_____

_____

- -

_____

_____

- -

_____

Name _____

When she was angry, her little eyes flashed blue.

The wrinkles of contempt crossed the wrinkles of peevishness, and made her face as full of wrinkles as a pat of butter.

Narration

From *The Light Princess*, by George MacDonald

What is one thing you remember about the passage?

_____

_____

_____

_____

_____

_____

_____

_____

_____

_____

_____

_____

_____

_____

_____

They soon found out that the princess was missing.

The wind carried her off through the opposite window
and away.

Narration and Copywork

From *The Light Princess*, by George MacDonald

What is one thing you remember about the passage?

Instructor

_____

- -

_____

_____

- -

_____

_____

- -

_____

Student

_____

- -

_____

_____

- -

_____

_____

- -

_____

A. A. Milne wrote stories about Piglet and Pooh.

The writer A. A. Milne really did have a son named
Christopher Robin.

Narration

From *A Child's Geography of the World,* by V. M. Hillyer

What is one thing you remember about the passage?

_____

_____

_____

_____

_____

_____

_____

_____

_____

_____

V. M. Hillyer wrote a book about geography for children.

V. M. Hillyer thought that children should also study maps, collect stamps, and make scrapbooks about the world.

Name _____

Narration and Copywork

From *A Child's Geography of the World,* by V. M. Hillyer

What is one thing you remember about the passage?

Instructor

_____

- -

_____

- -

_____

_____

- -

_____

Student

_____

- -

_____

- -

_____

- -

_____

_____

- -

_____

Copywork

My full name is _____ _____ _____.
　　　　　　　　　　(first name)　　　　　　(middle name)　　　　　　(last name)

My initials are _____ _____ _____.
　　　　　　　(first initial)　(middle initial)　(last initial)

My parent's full name is _____ _____ _____.
　　　　　　　　　　　　　(first name)　　　　　(middle name)　　　　　(last name)

My parent's initials are _____ _____ _____.
　　　　　　　　　　　(first initial)　(middle initial)　(last initial)

Name _____

From *Tom Sawyer,* by Mark Twain

What is one thing you remember about the passage?

Name _____

Jim came skipping out at the gate with a tin pail.

Saturday morning was come, and all the summer world was bright and fresh, and brimming with life.

Name _____

Narration and Copywork

From *Tom Sawyer,* by Mark Twain

What is one thing you remember about the passage?

Instructor

Student

They played in the garden in spring.

In spring, the boy and the rabbit spent long days in
the garden.

Narration

From *The Velveteen Rabbit*, by Margery Williams Bianco

What is one thing you remember about the passage?

_____

_____

_____

_____

_____

_____

_____

_____

_____

_____

_____

That was a wonderful summer.

In the spring, the boy went out to play in the wood.

Date _____

Name _____

Narration and Copywork

From *The Velveteen Rabbit*, by Margery Williams Bianco

What is one thing you remember about the passage?

Instructor

Student

Copywork

Billy dangled a leaf in front of the cat.

Joe came scuffing up the walk and flopped down beside Billy.

Date _____

Name _____

Narration

From *How to Eat Fried Worms,* by Thomas Rockwell

What is one thing you remember about the passage?

_____

- -

_____

_____

- -

_____

_____

- -

_____

_____

- -

_____

_____

- -

_____

_____

- -

_____

Name _____

And I will not eat them all at once.

Last week I put in the five dollars my grandmother gave me.

Narration and Copywork

From *How to Eat Fried Worms*, by Thomas Rockwell

What is one thing you remember about the passage?

Instructor

_____

- -

_____

- -

_____

_____

- -

_____

Student

_____

- -

_____

_____

- -

_____

_____

- -

_____

_____

- -

_____

Copywork

January . . . .

February . . . . . .

March . . . .

April . . . .

May (we do not
abbreviate May)

June . . . .

July . . . .

August . . . .

September . . . . .

October . . . .

November . . . . . .

December . . . . . .

Narration

From *The Happy Hollisters,* by Jerry West

What is one thing you remember about the passage?

Name _____

Copywork

Today is _____, _____ _____, _____.
   (day of the week)   (month) (day) (year)

Today is _____, _____ _____, _____.
   (day of the week) (month abbrev.) (day) (year)

I was born on _____ _____, _____.
      (month)   (day) (year)

I was born on _____ _____, _____.
     (month abbrev.) (day) (year)

Name _____

Narration and Copywork

From *The Happy Hollisters*, by Jerry West

What is one thing you remember about the passage?

Instructor

Student

Copywork

Now sit down, please, right here.

She used to come and sit on our doorstep with the kids.

From *Pollyanna*, by Eleanor Porter

What is one thing you remember about the passage?

_____

Name _____

She set the pitcher down at once.

Pollyanna was disappointed, and she set the bowl of jelly down.

Narration and Copywork

From *Pollyanna,* by Eleanor Porter

What is one thing you remember about the passage?

Instructor

_____

- -

_____

_____

- -

_____

_____

- -

_____

Student

_____

- -

_____

_____

- -

_____

_____

- -

_____

Copywork

From here they looked down into the garden of Mr. McGregor.

The gig was driven by Mr. McGregor, and beside him sat Mrs. McGregor in her best bonnet.

Narration

From *The Tale of Benjamin Bunny*, by Beatrix Potter

What is one thing you remember about the passage?

_____

_____

_____

_____

_____

_____

_____

_____

_____

_____

_____

_____

Old Mrs. Rabbit was a widow.

The name of the father of Benjamin was Mr. Benjamin Bunny.

Name _____

Narration and Copywork

From *The Tale of Benjamin Bunny*, by Beatrix Potter

What is one thing you remember about the passage?

Instructor

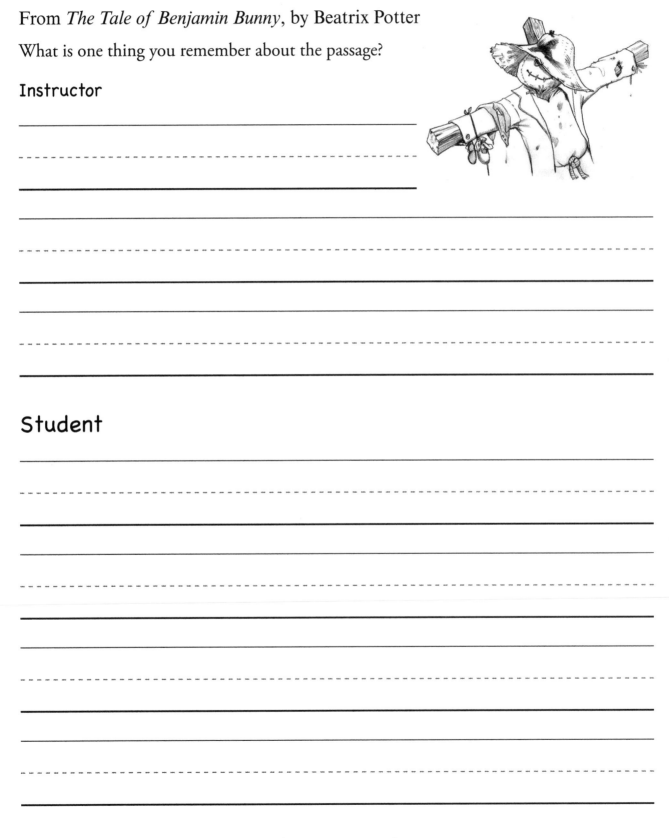

Student

Copywork

In came Mrs. Fezziwig, one vast substantial smile.

I have the pleasure of addressing Mr. Scrooge and Mr. Marley.

Date _____

Name _____

Narration

From *A Christmas Carol*, by Charles Dickens

What is one thing you remember about the passage?

_____

Mr. Scrooge it was.

In came the three Miss Fezziwigs, beaming and lovable.

Narration and Copywork

From *A Christmas Carol*, by Charles Dickens

What is one thing you remember about the passage?

Instructor

_____

- -

_____

_____

- -

_____

- -

_____

Student

_____

- -

_____

_____

- -

_____

_____

- -

_____

_____

- -

_____

Copywork

In the morning Mr. Scott slid down the rope and dug.

The buckets came up full of mud, and Pa and Mr. Scott worked every day in deeper mud.

Name _____

From *Little House on the Prairie,* by Laura Ingalls Wilder

What is one thing you remember about the passage?

Copywork

Grasshoppers beat down from the sky and swarmed thick over the ground.

Millions and millions of grasshoppers were eating now. You could hear the millions of jaws biting and chewing.

Narration and Copywork

From *On the Banks of Plum Creek,* by Laura Ingalls Wilder

What is one thing you remember about the passage?

Instructor

Student

Copywork

I am Miss Allen, your new librarian.

_____

- -

_____

_____

- -

_____

_____

- -

_____

You know how Tillie never takes a book out herself, but she is always wanting to read mine.

_____

- -

_____

_____

- -

_____

_____

- -

_____

Narration

From *All-of-a-Kind Family,* by Sydney Taylor

What is one thing you remember about the passage?

_____

Sarah studied the new library lady anxiously.

She has dimples, Sarah thought. Surely a lady with dimples could never be harsh.

Narration and Copywork

From *All-of-a-Kind Family*, by Sydney Taylor

What is one thing you remember about the passage?

Instructor

Student

Copywork

Splash, splash, splash, went her tears again.

_____

- -

_____

- -

_____

- -

_____

Once upon a time there was a deep and wide river, and in this river lived a crocodile.

_____

- -

_____

- -

_____

- -

_____

Narration

From *The Giant Crab and Other Tales from Old India*, retold by W. H. D. Rouse

What is one thing you remember about the passage?

_____

_____

_____

_____

_____

_____

_____

_____

_____

_____

_____

_____

Copywork

W. H. D. Rouse wrote new versions of many Jataka Tales.

_____

_____

_____

_____

W. H. D. Rouse, along with T. E. Page, edited a series of famous books about classic works of literature.

_____

_____

_____

_____

Name _____

Narration and Copywork

From *The Giant Crab and Other Tales from Old India,* retold by W. H. D. Rouse.

What is one thing you remember about the passage?

Instructor

Student

Copywork

Across the lonely beach we flit,

One little sandpiper and I,

And fast I gather' bit by bit,

The scattered driftwood, bleached and dry.

Narration

From "The Sandpiper," by Celia Thaxter

What is one thing you remember about the passage?

_____

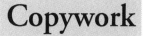

A nightingale, that all day long

Had cheered the village with his song,

Nor yet at eve his note suspended,

Nor yet when eventide was ended,

Began to feel, as well he might,

The keen demands of appetite.

Name _____

Narration and Copywork

From "The Nightingale and the Glow-worm," by William Cowper

What is one thing you remember about the passage?

Instructor

Student

Name _____

Come now and deal the stroke.

Take now the axe and let us see how well you can smite.

Narration

From *King Arthur and His Knights of the Round Table,* by Roger Lancelyn Green

What is one thing you remember about the passage?

_____

- -

_____

- -

_____

- -

_____

- -

_____

- -

_____

_____

- -

_____

- -

_____

Name _____

Noble uncle, let this adventure be mine.

See to it that you keep your oath and seek me out a year hence.

Name _____

Narration and Copywork

From *King Arthur and His Knights of the Round Table,* by Roger Lancelyn Green

What is one thing you remember about the passage?

Instructor

_____

- -

_____

_____

- -

_____

_____

- -

_____

Student

_____

- -

_____

_____

- -

_____

_____

- -

_____

_____

- -

_____

Have I ever told you about Willy Wonka?

Is it true that his chocolate factory is the biggest in the world?

Name _____

Narration

From *Charlie and the Chocolate Factory,* by Roald Dahl

What is one thing you remember about the passage?

_____

_____

_____

_____

_____

_____

_____

_____

_____

_____

_____

_____

Copywork

Did Mr. Wonka do it?

_____

_____

_____

_____

_____

_____

Have you ever seen a single person going into that place or coming out?

_____

_____

_____

_____

_____

_____

_____

_____

Narration and Copywork

From *Charlie and the Chocolate Factory,* by Roald Dahl

What is one thing you remember about the passage?

Instructor

Student

Name _____

Mommy, he hit me!

Okay, you win this time, but next time, look out!

Narration

From *Socks,* by Beverly Cleary

What is one thing you remember about the passage?

_____

- -

_____

_____

- -

_____

_____

- -

_____

_____

- -

_____

_____

- -

_____

_____

- -

_____

- - - - - - - - - - - - - - - - - - -

_____

_____

- - - - - - - - - - - - - - - - - - -

_____

_____

Name _____

Mommy, Socks likes me!

My, you are a big handsome boy with a nice thick coat!

Narration and Copywork

From *Socks,* by Beverly Cleary

What is one thing you remember about the passage?

Instructor

_____

- -

_____

_____

- -

_____

_____

- -

_____

Student

_____

- -

_____

_____

- -

_____

_____

- -

_____

_____

- -

_____

Copywork

Is the river so nice as all that?

_____

- -

_____

_____

- -

_____

_____

- -

_____

If you have nothing else on hand this morning, supposing we
drop down the river together, and have a long day of it?

_____

- -

_____

_____

- -

_____

_____

- -

_____

Date _____

Name _____

Narration

From *The Wind in the Willows*, by Kenneth Grahame

What is one thing you remember about the passage?

_____

Name _____

This has been a wonderful day!

How black was his despair when he felt himself sinking again!

Name _____

Narration and Copywork

From *The Wind in the Willows*, by Kenneth Grahame

What is one thing you remember about the passage?

Instructor

_____

_____

_____

_____

Student

_____

_____

_____

_____

_____

Mastery Evaluation Page 1
Copywork

The rain is falling all around,
It falls on field and tree,
It rains on the umbrellas here,
And on the ships at sea.

From *A Child's Garden of Verses,* by Robert Louis Stevenson

From *The Wonderful Wizard of Oz,* by L. Frank Baum

What is one thing you remember about the passage?

Mastery Evaluation Page 3
Copywork

L. Frank Baum wrote stories about a little girl who lived in Kansas. Her name was Dorothy, and she went to the land of Oz.

Name _____

From *The Wonderful Wizard of Oz,* by L. Frank Baum
What is one thing you remember about the passage?

Instructor

_____

- -

_____

- -

_____

- -

_____

Student

_____

- -

_____

- -

_____

- -

_____

DATE DUE

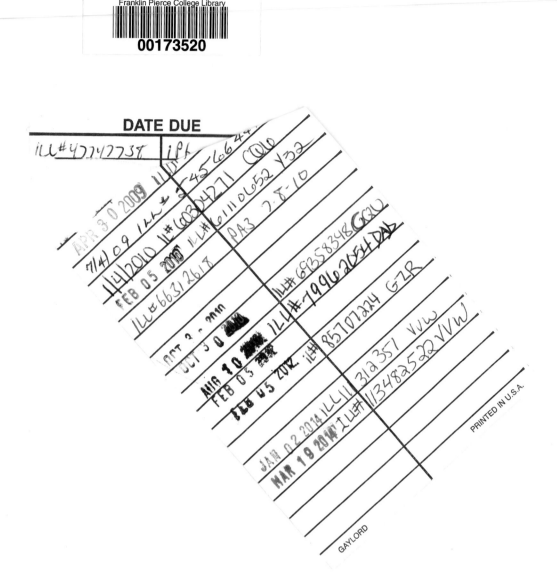

ILL#47747738   ipt

APR 3 0 2009   ILL# 45606249

7/4/09 ILL#603U4271   CDLO

11/4/2010   ILL#61110652 Y32

FEB 05 2010   PA3 2.8-10

ILL#66312618

OCT 3 0 2010   ILL#6858348 GGU

ILL#79962654 DAL

AUG 10   ILL#85707224 GZR

FEB 05 2012

JAN 02 2014   ILL#312357 VVW

MAR 19 2014   ILL#13482522 VVW

PRINTED IN U.S.A.

GAYLORD